A GREAT EMERGENCY

AND OTHER TALES

JULIANA HORATIA EWING

1st WORLD
LIBRARY
Literary Society

A Great Emergency and Other Tales

Juliana Horatia Ewing

© 1st World Library, 2007
PO Box 2211
Fairfield, IA 52556
www.1stworldlibrary.com
First Edition

LCCN: 2007934151

Softcover ISBN: 978-1-4218-9655-7
Hardcover ISBN: 978-1-4218-9755-4
eBook ISBN: 978-1-4218-9555-0

Purchase *"A Great Emergency and Other Tales"*
as a traditional bound book at:
www.1stWorldLibrary.com/purchase.asp?ISBN=978-1-4218-9655-7

1st World Library is a literary, educational organization
dedicated to:

- Creating a free internet library of downloadable ebooks

- Hosting writing competitions and offering book publishing
  scholarships.

Interested in more 1st World Library books? contact:
literacy@1stworldlibrary.com
Check us out at: www.1stworldlibrary.com

1st World Library Literary Society

Giving Back to the World

"If you want to work on the core problem, it's early school literacy."

- James Barksdale, former CEO of Netscape

"No skill is more crucial to the future of a child, or to a democratic and prosperous society, than literacy."

- Los Angeles Times

"Literacy... means far more than learning how to read and write... The aim is to transmit... knowledge and promote social participation."

- UNESCO

"Literacy is not a luxury, it is a right and a responsibility. If our world is to meet the challenges of the twenty-first century we must harness the energy and creativity of all our citizens."

- President Bill Clinton

"Parents should be encouraged to read to their children, and teachers should be equipped with all available techniques for teaching literacy, so the varying needs and capacities of individual kids can be taken into account."

- Hugh Mackay

DEDICATED TO

JOHN,

LORD BISHOP OF FREDERICTON,

AND TO HIS DEAR WIFE

MARGARET,

IN PLEASANT AND GRATEFUL MEMORY OF

NEW BRUNSWICK,

BY J.H.E.

CONTENTS

A VERY ILL-TEMPERED FAMILY

A GREAT EMERGENCY

CHAPTER I

RUPERT'S LECTURES—
THE OLD YELLOW LEATHER BOOK

We were very happy—I, Rupert, Henrietta, and Baby Cecil. The only thing we found fault with in our lives was that there were so few events in them.

It was particularly provoking, because we were so well prepared for events—any events. Rupert prepared us. He had found a fat old book in the garret, bound in yellow leather, at the end of which were "Directions how to act with presence of mind in any emergency;" and he gave lectures out of this in the kitchen garden.

Rupert was twelve years old. He was the eldest. Then came Henrietta, then I, and last of all Baby Cecil, who was only four. The day I was nine years old, Rupert came into the nursery, holding up his handsome head with the dignified air which became him so well, that I had more than once tried to put it on myself before the nursery looking-glass, and said to me, "You are quite old enough now, Charlie, to learn what to do whatever happens; so every half-holiday, when I am not playing cricket, I'll teach you presence of mind near the cucumber frame, if you're punctual. I've put up a bench."

I thanked him warmly, and the next day he put his head into the nursery at three o'clock in the afternoon, and said—"The lecture."

I jumped up, and so did Henrietta.

"It's not for girls," said Rupert; "women are not expected to do things when there's danger."

"*We* take care of *them*" said I, wondering if my mouth looked like Rupert's when I spoke, and whether my manner impressed Henrietta as much as his impressed me. She sat down again and only said, "I stayed in all Friday afternoon, and worked in bed on Saturday morning to finish your net."

"Come along," said Rupert. "You know I'm very much obliged to you for the net; it's a splendid one."

"I'll bring a camp-stool if there's not room on the bench," said Henrietta cheerfully.

"People never take camp-stools to lectures," said Rupert, and when we got to the cucumber frame we found that the old plank, which he had raised on inverted flower-pots, would have held a much larger audience than he had invited. Opposite to it was a rhubarb-pot, with the round top of a barrel resting on it. On this stood a glass of water. A delightful idea thrilled through me, suggested by an imperfect remembrance of a lecture on chemistry which I had attended.

"Will there be experiments?" I whispered.

"I think not," Henrietta replied. "There are glasses of water at the missionary meetings, and there are no experiments."

Meanwhile Rupert had been turning over the leaves of the yellow leather book. To say the truth, I think he was rather nervous; but if we have a virtue among us it is that of courage; and after dropping the book twice, and drinking all the water at a draught, he found his place, and began.

"*How to act in an emergency.*"

"What's an emergency?" I asked. I was very proud of being taught by Rupert, and anxious to understand everything as we went along.

"You shouldn't interrupt," said Rupert, frowning. I am inclined now to think that he could not answer my question off-hand; for though he looked cross then, after referring to the book he answered me: "It's a fire, or drowning, or an apoplectic fit, or anything of that sort." After which explanation, he hurried on. If what he said next came out of his own head, or whether he had learned it by heart, I never knew.

"There is no stronger sign of good-breeding than presence of mind in an—"

"—apoplectic fit," I suggested. I was giving the keenest attention, and Rupert had hesitated, the wind having blown over a leaf too many of the yellow leather book.

"An *emergency*," he shouted, when he had found his place. "Now we'll have one each time. The one for to-day is—How to act in a case of drowning."

To speak the strict truth, I would rather not have thought about drowning. I had my own private horror over a neighbouring mill-dam, and I had once been very much frightened by a spring-tide at the sea; but cowardice is not an indulgence for one of my race, so I screwed up my lips and pricked my ears to learn my duty in the unpleasant emergency of drowning.

"It doesn't mean being drowned yourself," Rupert continued, "but what to do when another person has been drowned."

The emergency was undoubtedly easier, and I gave a cheerful attention as Rupert began to question us.

"Supposing a man had been drowned in the canal, and was brought ashore, and you were the only people there, what would you do with him?"

I was completely nonplussed. "I felt quite sure I could do nothing with him, he would be so heavy; but I felt equally certain that this was not the answer which Rupert expected, so I left the question to Henrietta's readier wit. She knitted her thick eyebrows for some minutes, partly with perplexity, and partly because of the sunshine reflected from the cucumber frame, and then said,

"We should bury him in a vault; Charlie and I *couldn't* dig a grave deep enough."

I admired Henrietta's foresight, but Rupert was furious.

"How *silly* you are!" he exclaimed, knocking over the top of the rhubarb-pot table and the empty glass in his wrath. "Of course I don't mean a dead man. I mean what would you do to bring a partly drowned man to life again?"

"That wasn't what you *said*," cried Henrietta, tossing her head.

Juliana Horatia Ewing

"I let you come to my lecture," grumbled Rupert bitterly, as he stooped to set his table right, "and this is the way you behave!"

"I'm very sorry, Rupert dear!" said Henrietta. "Indeed, I only mean to do my best, and I do like your lecture so very much!"

"So do I," I cried, "very, very much!" And by a simultaneous impulse Henrietta and I both clapped our hands vehemently. This restored Rupert's self-complacency, and he bowed and continued the lecture. From this we learned that the drowned man should be turned over on his face to let the canal water run out of his mouth and ears, and that his wet clothes should be got off, and he should be made dry and warm as quickly as possible, and placed in a comfortable position, with the head and shoulders slightly raised. All this seemed quite feasible to us. Henrietta had dressed and undressed lots of dolls, and I pictured myself filling a hot-water bottle at the kitchen boiler with an air of responsibility that should scare all lighter-minded folk. But the directions for "restoring breathing" troubled our sincere desire to learn; and this even though Henrietta practised for weeks afterwards upon me. I represented the drowned man, and she drew my arms above my head for "*inspiration*," and counted "one, two;" and doubled them and drove them back for "*expiration*;" but it tickled, and I laughed, and we could not feel at all sure that it would have made the drowned man breathe again.

Meanwhile Rupert went on with the course of lectures, and taught us how to behave in the event of a fire in the house, an epidemic in the neighbourhood, a bite from a mad dog, a chase by a mad bull, broken limbs, runaway horses, a chimney on fire, or a young lady burning to death. The lectures were not only delightful in themselves, but they furnished us with a whole set of new games, for Henrietta and I zealously practised every emergency as far as the nature of things would allow. Covering our faces with wet cloths to keep off the smoke, we crept on our hands and knees to rescue a fancy cripple from an imaginary burning house, because of the current of air which Rupert told us was to be found near the floor. We fastened Baby Cecil's left leg to his right by pocket-handkerchiefs at the ankle, and above and below the knee, pretending that it was broken, and must be kept steady till we could convey him to the doctor. But for some unexplained reason Baby Cecil took offence at this game, and I do not think he could have howled and roared louder under the worst of real compound fractures. We had done it so skilfully, that we were greatly disgusted by his unaccommodating spirit, and his obstinate refusal to be put into the litter we had made out of Henrietta's stilts and a railway rug. We put the Scotch terrier in instead; but when one end of the litter gave way and he fell out, we were not sorry that the emergency was a fancy one, and that no broken limbs were really dependent upon our well-meant efforts.

There was one thing about Rupert's lectures which disappointed me. His emergencies were all things that happened in the daytime. Now I should not have liked the others to know that I was ever afraid of anything; but, really and truly, I was sometimes a little frightened—not of breaking my leg, or a house on fire, or an apoplectic fit, or anything of that sort, but—of things in the dark. Every half-holiday I hoped there would be something about what to do with robbers or ghosts, but there never was. I do not think there can have been any emergencies of that kind in the yellow leather book.

On the whole, I fancy Rupert found us satisfactory pupils, for he never did give up the lectures in a huff, though he sometimes threatened to do so, when I asked stupid questions, or Henrietta argued a point.

Juliana Horatia Ewing

CHAPTER II

HENRIETTA—A FAMILY CHRONICLE—
THE SCHOOL MIMIC—MY FIRST FIGHT

Henrietta often argued points, which made Rupert very angry. He said that even if she were in the right, that had nothing to do with it, for girls oughtn't to dispute or discuss. And then Henrietta argued that point too.

Rupert and Henrietta often squabbled, and always about the same sort of thing. I am sure he would have been *very* kind to her if she would have agreed with him, and done what he wanted. He often told me that the gentlemen of our family had always been courteous to women, and I think he would have done anything for Henrietta if it had not been that she would do everything for herself.

When we wanted to vex her very much, we used to call her "Monkey," because we knew she liked to be like a boy. She persuaded Mother to let her have her boots made like ours, because she said the roads were so rough and muddy (which they are). And we found two of her books with her name written in, and she had put "Henry," and Rupert wrote Etta after it, and "Monkey" after that. So she tore the leaves out. Her hair was always coming out of curl. It was very dark, and when it fell into her eyes she used to give her head a peculiar shake and toss, so that half of it fell the wrong way, and there was a parting at the side, like our partings. Nothing made Rupert angrier than this.

Henrietta was very good at inventing things. Once she invented a charade quite like a story. Rupert was very much pleased with it, because he was to act the hero, who was to be a young cavalier of a very old family—our family. He was to arrive at an inn; Henrietta made it the real old inn in the middle of the town, and I was the innkeeper, with Henrietta's pillow to make me fat, and one of Nurse's clean aprons. Then he was to ask to spend a night in the old Castle, and Henrietta made that the real Castle, which was about nine miles off, and which belonged to our cousin, though he never spoke to us. And a ghost was to appear. The ghost of the ancestor in the miniature in Mother's bedroom. Henrietta did the ghost in a white sheet; and with her hair combed, and burnt-cork moustache, she looked so exactly like the picture that Rupert started when she came in, and stared; and Mother said he had acted splendidly.

Henrietta was wonderfully like the picture. Much more like than Rupert ever was, which rather vexed him, because that ancestor was one of the very bravest, and his name was Rupert. He was rather vexed, too, when she rode the pony bare-backed which had kicked him off. But I think the pony was fonder of Henrietta, which perhaps made it easier for her to manage it. She used to feed it with bits of bread. It got them out of her pocket.

One of the things Henrietta could not do as well as Rupert was cricket. Rupert was one of the best players in the school. Henrietta used to want to play with us at home, and she and I did play for a bit, before breakfast, in the drying ground; but Rupert said, if I encouraged her in being unladylike, he would not let me come to the school matches. He said I might take my choice, and play either with girls or boys, but not with both. But I thought it would be very mean to leave Henrietta in the lurch. So I told her I would stick by her, as Rupert had not actually forbidden me. He had given me my choice, and he always kept his word. But she would not let me. She pretended that she did not mind; but I know she did, for I could see afterwards that she had been crying. However, she would not play, and Mother said she had much rather she did not, as she was so afraid of her getting hit by the ball. So that settled it, and I was very glad not to have to give up going to the school matches.

The school we went to was the old town grammar school. It was a very famous one; but it was not so expensive as big public schools are, and I believe this was why we lived in this town after my father's death, for Mother was not at all rich.

The grammar school was very large, and there were all sorts of boys there—some of gentlemen, and tradesmen, and farmers. Some of the boys were so very dirty, and had such horrid habits out of school, that when Rupert was thirteen, and I was ten, he called a council at the beginning of the half, and a lot of the boys formed a committee, and drew up the code of honour, and we all subscribed to it.

The code of honour was to forbid a lot of things that had been very common in the school. Lying, cheating over bargains, telling tales, bragging, bad language, and what the code called "conduct unbecoming schoolfellows and gentlemen." There were a lot of rules in it, too, about clean nails, and shirts, and collars and socks, and things of that sort. If any boy refused to agree to it, he had to fight with Thomas Johnson.

There could not have been a better person than Rupert to

make a code of honour. We have always been taught that honour was the watch-word of our family—dearer than anything that could be gained or lost, very much dearer than mere life. The motto of our arms came from an ancestor who lost the favour of the King by refusing to do something against his conscience for which he would have been rewarded. It is "Honour before honours."

I can just remember the man, with iron-grey hair and gold spectacles, who came to our house after my father's death. I think he was a lawyer. He took lots of snuff, so that Henrietta sneezed when he kissed her, which made her very angry. He put Rupert and me in front of him, to see which of us was most like my father, and I can recall the big pinch of snuff he took, and the sound of his voice saying "Be like your father, boys! He was as good as he was gallant. And there never lived a more honourable gentleman."

Every one said the same. We were very proud of it, and always boasted about our father to the new nursemaids, or any other suitable hearer. I was a good deal annoyed by one little maid, who when I told her, over our nursery tea, that my father had been the most honourable of men, began to cry about her father, who was dead too, and said he was "just the same; for in the one and twenty years he kept a public-house, he never put so much as a pinch of salt into the beer, nor even a gill of water, unless it was in the evening at fair-time, when the only way to keep the men from fighting was to give them their liquor so that it could not do them much harm." I was very much offended by the comparison of *my* father, who was an officer and a gentleman of rank, with *her* father, who was a village publican; but I should like to say, that I think now that I was wrong and Jane was right. If her father gave up profit for principle, he *was* like my father, and like the ancestor we get the motto from, and like every other honourable man, of any rank or any trade.

Every time I boasted in the nursery of my father being so honourable, I always finished my saying, that that was why he had the word Honourable before his name, as men in old times used to be called "the Good" or "the Lion Heart." The nursemaids quite believed it, and I believed it myself, till the first week I went to school.

It makes me hot all over to remember what I suffered that week, and for long, afterwards. But I think it cured me of bragging, which is a mean ungentlemanly habit, and of telling everybody everything about myself and my relations, which is very weak-minded.

The second day I was there, one of the boys came up to me and said, with a mock ceremony and politeness which unfortunately took me in, "If I am not mistaken, sir, that esteemed lady, your mother, is an Honourable?"

He was nearly five years older than I; his name was Weston; he had a thin cadaverous face, a very large nose, and a very melancholy expression. I found out afterwards that he was commonly called "the clown," and was considered by boys who had been to the London theatres to surpass the best professional comic actors when he chose to put forth his powers. I did not know this then. I thought him a little formal, but particularly courteous in his manner, and not wishing to be behindhand in politeness, I replied, with as much of his style as I could assume, "Certainly, sir. But that is because my father was an Honourable. My father, sir, was the most honourable of men."

A slight spasm appeared to pass over Weston's face, and then he continued the conversation in a sadder tone than the subject seemed to require, but I supposed that this was due to his recalling that my father was dead.

I confess that it did not need many leading inquiries to draw from me such a narrative of my father's valour and high principle, as well as the noble sentiments and conspicuous bravery which have marked our family from Saxon times, as I was well accustomed to pour forth for the edification of our nursemaids. I had not proceeded far, when my new friend said, "Won't you walk in and take a seat?" It was recreation time, and the other boys were all out in the playground. I had no special friend as yet; Rupert had stuck to me all the first day, and had now left me to find my own level. I had lingered near the door as we came out, and there Weston had joined me. He now led me back into the deserted school-room, and we sat down together on an old black oak locker, at the bottom of the room.

How well I remember the scene! The dirty floor, the empty benches, the torn books sprinkled upon the battered desks, the dusty sunshine streaming in, the white-faced clock on the wall opposite, over which the hands moved with almost incredible rapidity. But when does time ever fly so fast as with people who are talking about themselves or their relations?

Once the mathematical master passed through the room. He glanced at us curiously, but Weston's face was inscrutable, and I—tracing some surprise that I should have secured so old and so fine-mannered a boy for a friend—held up my head, and went on with my narrative, as fluently as I could, to show that I had parts which justified Weston in his preference.

Tick, tack! went the clock. Click, clack! went my tongue. I fear that quite half-an-hour must have passed, when a big boy, with an open face, blue eyes, and closely curling fair hair, burst in. On seeing us he exclaimed, "Hulloh!" and then stopped, I suspect in obedience to Weston's eyes, which met his in a brief but expressive gaze. Then Weston turned to me.

"Allow me," said he, "to introduce Mr. Thomas Johnson. He bears a very high character in this school, and it will afford him the keenest satisfaction to hear an authentic account of such a man as your esteemed father, whose character should be held up for the imitation of young gentlemen in every establishment for the education of youth."

I blushed with pride and somewhat with nervousness as Mr. Thomas Johnson seated himself on the locker on the other side of me and begged (with less elegance of expression than my first friend) that I would "go ahead."

I did so. But a very few minutes exhausted the patience of my new hearer. When he had kicked a loose splinter of wood satisfactorily off the leg of one of the desks he began to look at the clock, which quickened my pace from my remoter ancestors to what the colonel of the regiment in which my father was an ensign had said of him. I completed my narrative at last with the lawyer's remark, and added, "and everybody says the same. And *that* is why my father had '*The Honourable*' before his name, just as—" &c., &c.

I had no sooner uttered these words than Johnson started from his seat, and, covering his face with a spotted silk pocket-handkerchief, rushed precipitately from the school-room. For one brief instant I fancied I heard him choking with laughter, but when I turned to Weston he got up too, with a look of deep concern. "Mr. Johnson is taken very unwell, I fear," said he. "It is a peculiar kind of spasm to which he is subject. Excuse me!"

He hurried anxiously after his friend, and I was left alone in the school-room, into which the other boys shortly began to pour.

"Have you been all alone, old fellow?" said Rupert kindly; "I hoped you had picked up a chum."

"So I have," was my proud reply; "two chums."

"I hope they're decent fellows," said Rupert. (He had a most pestilent trick of perpetually playing monitor, to the wet-blanketing of all good fellowship.)

"You know best," said I pertly; "it's Weston and Johnson. We've been together a long time."

"Weston?" cried Rupert. "I hope to goodness, Charlie, you've not been playing the fool?"

"You can ask them," said I, and tossing my head I went to my proper place.

For the rest of school-time I wore a lofty and Rupert an anxious demeanour. Secure on the level of a higher friendship, I was mean enough to snub the friendly advances of one or two of the younger boys.

When we went home at night, I found my mother much more ready than Rupert to believe that my merits had gained for me the regard of two of the upper boys. I was exultingly happy. Not a qualm disturbed the waking dreams in which (after I was in bed) I retold my family tale at even greater length than before, except that I remembered one or two incidents, which in the excitement of the hour I had forgotten when in school.

I was rather sorry, too, that, bound by the strictest of injunctions from Rupert and my own promise, I had not been able, ever so casually, to make my new friends aware that among my other advantages was that of being first cousin to a peer, the very one who lived at the Castle. The Castle was a show place, and I knew that many of my schoolfellows were glad enough to take their friends and go themselves to be shown by the housekeeper the pictures of *my* ancestors. On this point they certainly had an advantage over me. I had not seen the pictures. Our cousin never called on us, and never asked us to the Castle, and of course we could not go to our father's old home like common holiday-making townspeople.

I would rather not say very much about the next day. It must seem almost incredible that I could have failed to see that Weston and Johnson were making fun of me; and I confess that it was not for want of warnings that I had made a fool of myself.

I had looked forward to going to school with about equal measures of delight and dread; my pride and ambition longed for this first step in life, but Rupert had filled me with a wholesome awe of its stringent etiquette, its withering ridicule, and unsparing severities. However, in his anxiety to make me modest and circumspect, I think he rather over-painted the picture, and when I got through the first day without being bullied, and made such creditable friends on the second, I began to think that Rupert's experience of school life must be due to some lack of those social and conversational powers with which I seemed to be better endowed. And then Weston's acting would have deceived a wiser head than mine. And the nursemaids had always listened so willingly!

As it happened, Rupert was unwell next day and could not go to school. He was obviously afraid of my going alone, but I had no fears. My self-satisfaction was not undone till playtime. Then not a boy dispersed to games. They all gathered round Weston in the playground, and with a confident air I also made my way to his side. As he turned his face to me I was undeceived.

Weston was accustomed—at such times as suited his caprice and his resources—to give exhibitions of his genius for mimicry to the rest of the boys. I had heard from Rupert of these entertainments, which were much admired by the school. They commonly consisted of funny dialogues between various worthies of the place well known to everybody, which made Weston's audience able to judge of the accuracy of his imitations. From the head-master to the idiot who blew the organ bellows in church, every inhabitant of the place who was gifted with any recognizable peculiarity was personated at one time or another by the wit of our school. The favourite imitation of all was supposed to be one of the Dialogues of Plato, "omitted by some strange over-sight in, the edition which graces the library of our learned and respected doctor," Weston would say with profound gravity. The Dialogue was between Dr. Jessop and Silly Billy—the idiot already referred to—and the apposite Latin quotations of the head-master and his pompous English, with the inapposite replies of the organ-blower, given in the local dialect and Billy's own peculiar jabber, were supposed to form a masterpiece of mimicry.

Little did I think that my family chronicle was to supply Weston with a new field for his talents!

In the midst of my shame, I could hardly help admiring the clever way in which he had remembered all the details, and twisted them into a comic ballad, which he had composed overnight, and which he now recited with a mock heroic air and voice, which made every point tell, and kept the boys in convulsions of laughter. Not a smile crossed his long, lantern-jawed face; but Mr. Thomas Johnson made no effort this time to hide a severe fit of his peculiar spasms in his spotted handkerchief.

Sometimes—at night—in the very bottom of my own heart,

Juliana Horatia Ewing

when the darkness seemed thick with horrors, and when I could not make up my mind whether to keep my ears strained to catch the first sound of anything dreadful, or to pull the blankets over my head and run the risk of missing it,—in such moments, I say, I have had a passing private doubt whether I had inherited my share of the family instinct of courage at a crisis.

It was therefore a relief to me to feel that in this moment of despair, when I was only waiting till the boys, being no longer amused by Weston, should turn to amuse themselves with me, my first and strongest feeling was a sense of relief that Rupert was not at school, and that I could bear the fruits of my own folly on my own shoulders. To be spared his hectoring and lecturing, his hurt pride, his reproaches, and rage with me, and a probable fight with Weston, in which he must have been seriously hurt and I should have been blamed—this was some comfort.

I had got my lesson well by heart. Fifty thousand preachers in fifty thousand pulpits could never have taught me so effectually as Weston's ballad, and the laughter of his audience, that there is less difference than one would like to believe between the vanity of bragging of one's self and the vanity of bragging of one's relations. Also that it is not dignified or discreet to take new acquaintance into your entire confidence and that even if one is blessed with friends of such quick sympathy that they really enjoy hearing about people they have never seen, it is well not to abuse the privilege, and now and then to allow them an "innings" at describing *their* remarkable parents, brothers, sisters, and remoter relatives.

I realized all this fully as I stood, with burning cheeks and downcast eyes, at the very elbow of my tormentor. But I am glad to know that I would not have run away even if I could.

My resolution grew stubborner with every peal of laughter to bear whatever might come with pluck and good temper. I had been a fool, but I would show that I was not a coward.

I was very glad that Rupert's influenza kept him at home for a few days. I told him briefly that I had been bullied, but that it was my own fault, and I would rather say no more about it. I begged him to promise that he would not take up my quarrel in any way, but leave me to fight it out for myself, which he did. When he came back I think he regretted his promise. Happily he never heard all the ballad, but the odd verses which the boys sang about the place put him into a fury. It was a long time before he forgave me, and I doubt if he ever quite forgave Weston.

I held out as well as I could. I made no complaint, and kept my temper. I must say that Henrietta behaved uncommonly well to me at this time.

"After all, you know, Charlie," she said, "you've not done anything *really wrong or dishonourable.*" This was true, and it comforted me.

Except Henrietta, I really had not a friend; for Rupert was angry with me, and the holding up at school only made me feel worse at home.

At last the joke began to die out, and I was getting on very well, but for one boy, a heavy-looking fellow with a pasty face, who was always creeping after me, and asking me to tell him about my father. "Johnson Minor," we called him. He was a younger brother of Thomas Johnson, the champion of the code of honour.

He was older than I, but he was below me in class, and though he was bigger, he was not a very great deal bigger;

and if there is any truth in the stories I have so often told, our family has been used to fight against odds for many generations.

I thought about this a good deal, and measured Johnson Minor with my eye. At last I got Henrietta to wrestle and box with me for practice.

She was always willing to do anything Tomboyish, indeed she was generally willing to do anything one wanted, and her biceps were as hard as mine, for I pinched them to see. We got two pairs of gloves, much too big for us, and stuffed cotton wool in to make them like boxing-gloves, as we used to stuff out the buff-coloured waistcoat when we acted old gentlemen in it. But it did not do much good; for I did not like to hurt Henrietta when I got a chance, and I do not think she liked to hurt me. So I took to dumb-belling every morning in my night-shirt; and at last I determined I would have it out with Johnson Minor, once for all.

One afternoon, when the boys had been very friendly with me, and were going to have me in the paper chase on Saturday, he came up in the old way and began asking me about my father, quite gravely, like a sort of poor imitation of Weston. So I turned round and said, "Whatever my father was—he's dead. Your father's alive, Johnson, and if you weren't a coward, you wouldn't go on bullying a fellow who hasn't got one."

"I'm a coward, am I, Master Honourable?" said Johnson, turning scarlet, and at the word *Honourable* I thought he had broken my nose. I never felt such pain in my life, but it was the only pain I felt on the occasion; afterwards I was much too much excited, I am sorry that I cannot remember very clearly about it, which I should have liked to do, as it was my first fight.

There was no time to fight properly. I was obliged to do the best I could. I made a sort of rough plan in my head, that I would cling to Johnson as long as I was able, and hit him whenever I got a chance. I did not quite know when he was hitting me from when I was hitting him; but I know that I held on, and that the ground seemed to be always hitting us both.

How long we had been struggling and cuffing and hitting (less scientifically but more effectually than when Henrietta and I flourished our stuffed driving gloves, with strict and constant reference to the woodcuts in a sixpenny Boxer's Guide) before I got slightly stunned, I do not know; when I came round I was lying in Weston's arms, and Johnson Minor was weeping bitterly (as he believed) over my corpse. I fear Weston had not allayed his remorse.

My great anxiety was to shake hands with Johnson. I never felt more friendly towards any one.

He met me in the handsomest way. He apologized for speaking of my father—"since you don't like it," he added, with an appearance of sincerity which puzzled me at the time, and which I did not understand till afterwards—and I apologized for calling him a coward. We were always good friends, and our fight made an end of the particular chaff which had caused it.

It reconciled Rupert to me too, which was my greatest gain.

Rupert is quite right. There is nothing like being prepared for emergencies. I suppose, as I was stunned, that Johnson got the best of it; but judging from his appearance as we washed ourselves at the school pump, I was now quite prepared for the emergency of having to defend myself against any boy not twice my own size.

Juliana Horatia Ewing

CHAPTER III

SCHOOL CRICKET—LEMON-KALI—THE BOYS' BRIDGE—AN UNEXPECTED EMERGENCY

Rupert and I were now the best of good friends again. I cared more for his favour than for the goodwill of any one else, and kept as much with him as I could.

I played cricket with him in the school matches. At least I did not bat or bowl, but I and some of the junior fellows "fielded out," and when Rupert was waiting for the ball, I would have given my life to catch quickly and throw deftly. I used to think no one ever looked so handsome as he did in his orange-coloured shirt, white flannel trousers, and the cap which Henrietta made him. He and I had spent all our savings on that new shirt, for Mother would not get him a new one. She did not like cricket, or anything at which people could hurt themselves. But Johnson Major had get a new sky-blue shirt and cap, and we did not like Rupert to be outdone by him, for Johnson's father is only a canal-carrier.

But the shirt emptied our pockets, and made the old cap look worse than ever. Then Henrietta, without saying a word to us, bought some orange flannel, and picked the old cap to pieces, and cut out a new one by it, and made it all herself, with a button, and a stiff peak and everything, and it really did perfectly, and looked very well in the sunshine over Rupert's brown face and glossy black hair.

There always was sunshine when we played cricket. The hotter it was the better we liked it. We had a bottle of lemon-kali powder on the ground, and I used to have to make a fizzing-cup in a tin mug for the other boys. I got the water from the canal.

Lemon-kali is delicious on a very hot day—so refreshing! But I sometimes fancied I felt a little sick *afterwards*, if I had had a great deal. And Bustard (who was always called Bustard-Plaster, because he was the doctor's son) said it was the dragons out of the canal water lashing their tails inside us. He had seen them under his father's microscope.

The field where we played was on the banks of the canal, the opposite side to the town. I believe it was school property. At any rate we had the right of playing there.

We had to go nearly a quarter of a mile out of the way before there was a bridge, and it was very vexatious to toil a quarter of a mile down on one side and a quarter of a mile up on the other to get at a meadow which lay directly opposite to the school. Weston wrote a letter about it to the weekly paper asking the town to build us a bridge. He wrote splendid letters, and this was one of his very best. He said that if the town council laughed at the notion of building a bridge for boys, they must remember that the Boys of to-day were the Men of to-morrow (which we all thought a grand sentence, though MacDonald, a very accurate-minded fellow, said it would really be some years before most of us were grown up). Then Weston called us the Rising Generation, and showed that, in all probability, the Prime Minister, Lord Chancellor, and Primate of the years to come now played "all unconscious of their future fame" in the classic fields that lay beyond the water, and promised that in the hours of our coming greatness we would look back with gratitude to the munificence of our native city. He put lots of Latin in, and ended with some Latin verses of his own, in which he made the Goddess of the Stream plead for us as her sons. By the stream he meant the canal, for we had no river, which of course Weston couldn't help.

How we watched for the next week's paper! But it wasn't in. They never did put his things in, which mortified him sadly. His greatest ambition was to get something of his own invention printed. Johnson said he believed it was because Weston always put something personal in the things he wrote. He was very sarcastic, and couldn't help making fun of people.

It was all the kinder of Weston to do his best about the bridge, because he was not much of a cricketer himself. He said he was too short-sighted, and that it suited him better to poke in the hedges for beetles. He had a splendid collection of insects. Bustard used to say that he poked with his nose, as if he were an insect himself, and it was a proboscis but he said too that his father said it was a pleasure to see Weston make a section of anything, and prepare objects for the microscope. His fingers were as clever as his tongue.

It was not long after Rupert got his new shirt and cap that a very sad thing happened.

We were playing cricket one day as usual. It was very hot, and I was mixing some lemon-kali at the canal, and holding up the mug to tempt Weston over, who was on the other side with his proboscis among the water-plants collecting larvae. Rupert was batting, and a new fellow, who bowled much more swiftly than we were accustomed to, had the ball. I was straining my ears to catch what Weston was shouting to me between his hands, when I saw him start and point to the cricketers, and turning round I saw Rupert lying on the ground.

The ball had hit him on the knee and knocked him down. He struggled up, and tried to stand; but whilst he was saying it was nothing, and scolding the other fellows for not going on, he fell down again fainting from pain.

"The leg's broken, depend upon it," said Bustard-Plaster; "shall I run for my father?"

I thanked him earnestly, for I did not like to leave Rupert myself. But Johnson Major, who was kicking off his cricketing-shoes, said, "It'll take an hour to get round. I'll go. Get him some water, and keep his cap on. The sun is blazing." And before we could speak he was in the canal and swimming across.

I went back to the bank for my mug, in which the lemon-kali was fizzing itself out, and with this I got some water for Rupert, and at last he opened his eyes. As I was getting the water I saw Weston, unmooring a boat which was fastened a little farther up. He was evidently coming to help us to get Rupert across the canal.

Bustard's words rang in my ears. Perhaps Rupert's leg was broken. Bustard was a doctor's son, and ought to know. And I have often thought it must be a very difficult thing *to* know, for people's legs don't break right off when they break. My first feeling had been utter bewilderment and misery, but I collected my senses with the reflection that if I lost my presence of mind in the first real emergency that happened to me, my attendance at Rupert's lectures had been a mockery, and I must be the first fool and coward of my family. And if I failed in the emergency of a broken leg, how could I ever hope to conduct myself with credit over a case of drowning? I did feel thankful that Rupert's welfare did not depend on our pulling his arms up and down in a particular way; but as Weston was just coming ashore, I took out my pocket-handkerchief, and kneeling down by Rupert said, with as good an air as I could assume, "We must tie the broken leg to the other at the—"

"*Don't touch it*, you young fool!" shrieked Rupert. And though directly afterwards he begged my pardon for speaking sharply, he would not hear of my touching his leg. So they got him into the boat the best way they could, and Weston sat by him to hold him up, and the boy who had been bowling pulled them across. I wasn't big enough to do either, so I had to run round by the bridge.

I fancy it must be easier to act with presence of mind if the emergency has happened to somebody who has not been used to order you about as much as Rupert was used to order me.

CHAPTER IV

A DOUBTFUL BLESSING—A FAMILY FAILING—
OLD BATTLES—THE CANAL-CARRIER'S HOME

When we found that Rupert's leg was not broken, and that it was only a severe blow on his knee, we were all delighted. But when weeks and months went by and he was still lame and very pale and always tired, we began to count for how long past, if the leg had been broken, it would have been set, and poor Rupert quite well. And when Johnny Bustard said that legs and arms were often stronger after being broken than before (if they were properly set, as his father could do them), we felt that if Gregory would bowl for people's shins he had better break them at once, and let Mr. Bustard make a good job of them.

The first part of the time Rupert made light of his accident, and wanted to go back to school, and was very irritable and impatient. But as the year went on he left off talking about its being all nonsense, and though he suffered a great deal he never complained. I used quite to miss his lecturing me, but he did not even squabble with Henrietta now.

This reminds me of a great fault of mine—I am afraid it was a family failing, though it is a very mean one—I was jealous. If I was "particular friends" with any one, I liked to have him

Juliana Horatia Ewing

all to myself; when Rupert was "out" with me because of the Weston affair, I was "particular friends" with Henrietta. I did not exactly give her up when Rupert and I were all right again, but when she complained one day (I think *she* was jealous too!) I said, "I'm particular friends with you *as a sister* still; but you know Rupert and I are both boys."

I did love Rupert very dearly, and I would have given up anything and everything to serve him and wait upon him now that he was laid up; but I would rather have had him all to myself, whereas Henrietta was now his particular friend. It is because I know how meanly I felt about it that I should like to say how good she was. My Mother was very delicate, and she had a horror of accidents; but Henrietta stood at Mr. Bustard's elbow all the time he was examining Rupert's knee, and after that she always did the fomentations and things. At first Rupert said she hurt him, and would have Nurse to do it; but Nurse hurt him so much more, that then he would not let anybody but Henrietta touch it. And he never called her Monkey now, and I could see how she tried to please him. One day she came down to breakfast with her hair all done up in the way that was in fashion then, like a grown-up young lady, and I think Rupert was pleased, though she looked rather funny and very red. And so Henrietta nursed him altogether, and used to read battles to him as he lay on the sofa, and Rupert made plans of the battles on cardboard, and moved bits of pith out of the elder-tree about for the troops, and showed Henrietta how if he had had the moving of them really, and had done it quite differently to the way the generals did, the other side would have won instead of being beaten.

And Mother used to say, "That's just the way your poor father used to go on! As if it wasn't enough to have to run the risk of being killed or wounded once or twice yourself, without bothering your head about battles you've nothing to do with."

And when he did the battle in which my father fell, and planted the battery against which he led his men for the last time, and where he was struck under the arm, with which he was waving his sword over his head, Rupert turned whiter than ever, and said, "Good Heavens, Henrietta! Father *limped* up to that battery! He led his men for two hours, after he was wounded in the leg, before he fell—and here I sit and grumble at a knock from a cricket-ball!"

Just then Mr. Bustard came in, and when he shook Rupert's hand he kept his fingers on it, and shook his own head; and he said there was "an abnormal condition of the pulse," in such awful tones, that I was afraid it was something that Rupert would die of. But Henrietta understood better, and she would not let Rupert do that battle any more.

Rupert's friends were very kind to him when he was ill, but the kindest of all was Thomas Johnson.

Johnson's grandfather was a canal-carrier, and made a good deal of money, and Johnson's father got the money and went on with the business. We had a great discussion once in the nursery as to whether Johnson's father was a gentleman, and Rupert ran down-stairs, and into the drawing-room, shouting, "Now, Mother! *is* a carrier a gentleman?"

And Mother, who was lying on the sofa, said, "Of course not. What silly things you children do ask! Why can't you amuse yourselves in the nursery? It is very hard you should come and disturb me for such a nonsensical question."

Rupert was always good to Mother, and he shut the drawing-room door very gently. Then he came rushing up to the nursery to say that Mother said "Of course not." But

Henrietta said, "What did you ask her?" And when Rupert told her she said, "Of course Mother thought you meant one of those men who have carts to carry things, with a hood on the top and a dog underneath."

Johnson's father and grandfather were not carriers of that kind. They owned a lot of canal-boats, and one or two big barges, which took all kinds of things all the way to London.

Mr. Johnson used to say, "In my father's time men of business lived near their work both in London and the country. That's why my house is close to the wharf. I am not ashamed of my trade, and the place is very comfortable, so I shall stick to it. Tom may move into the town and give the old house to the foreman when I am gone, if he likes to play the fine gentleman."

Tom would be very foolish if he did. It is the dearest old house one could wish for. It was built of red brick, but the ivy has covered it so thickly that it is clipped round the old-fashioned windows like a hedge. The gardens are simply perfect. In summer you can pick as many flowers and eat as much fruit as you like, and if that is not the use and beauty of a garden, I do not know what is.

Johnson's father was very proud of him, and let him have anything he liked, and in the midsummer holidays Johnson used to bring his father's trap and take Rupert out for drives, and Mrs. Johnson used to put meat pies and strawberries in a basket under the seat, so that it was a kind of picnic, for the old horse had belonged to Mr. Bustard, and was a capital one for standing still.

It was partly because of the Johnsons being so kind to Rupert that Johnson Minor and I became chums at school, and partly because the fight had made us friendly, and I had no Rupert now, and was rather jealous of his taking completely to Henrietta, and most of all, I fancy, because Johnson Minor was determined to be friends with me. He was a very odd fellow. There was nothing he liked so much as wonderful stories about people, and I never heard such wonderful stories as he told himself. When we became friends he told me that he had never meant to bully me when he asked about my father; he really did want to hear about his battles and so forth.

But the utmost I could tell him about my father was nothing to the tales he told me about his grandfather, the navy captain.

CHAPTER V

THE NAVY CAPTAIN—SEVEN PARROTS IN A FUCHSIA TREE—THE HARBOUR LION AND THE SILVER CHAIN—THE LEGLESS GIANTS—DOWN BELOW—JOHNSON'S WHARF

The Johnsons were very fond of their father, he was such a good, kind man; but I think they would have been glad if he had had a profession instead of being a canal-carrier, and I am sure it pleased them to think that Mrs. Johnson's father had been a navy captain, and that his portrait—uniform and all—hung over the horsehair sofa in the dining-room, near the window where the yellow roses used to come in.

If I could get the room to myself, I used to kneel on the sofa, on one of the bolsters, and gaze at the faded little picture till I lost my balance on the slippery horsehair from the intensity of my interest in the hero of Johnson Minor's tales. Every time, I think, I expected to see some change in the expression of the captain's red face, adapting it better to what, by his grandson's account, his character must have been. It seemed so odd he should look so wooden after having seen so much.

The captain had been a native of South Devon.

"Raleigh, Drake, my grandfather, and lots of other great

sailors were born in Devonshire," Johnson said. He certainly did brag; but he spoke so slowly and quietly, that it did not sound as like bragging as it would have done if he had talked faster, I think.

The captain had lived at Dartmouth, and of this place Johnson gave me such descriptions, that to this day the name of Dartmouth has a romantic sound in my ears, though I know now that all the marvels were Johnson's own invention, and barely founded upon the real quaintness of the place, of which he must have heard from his mother. It became the highest object of my ambition to see the captain's native city. That there must be people—shopkeepers, for instance, and a man to keep the post office—who lived there all along, was a fact that I could not realize sufficiently to envy them.

Johnson—or Fred, as I used to call him by this time—only exaggerated the truth about the shrubs that grow in the greenhouse atmosphere of South Devon, when he talked of the captain's fuchsia trees being as big as the old willows by the canal wharf; but the parrots must have been a complete invention. He said the captain had seven. Two green, two crimson, two blue, and one violet with an orange-coloured beak and grey lining to his wings; and that they built nests in the fuchsia trees of sandal-wood shavings, and lined them with the captain's silk pocket-handkerchiefs. He said that though the parrots stole the captain's handkerchiefs, they were all very much attached to him; but they quarrelled among themselves, and swore at each other in seven dialects of the West Coast of Africa.

Mrs. Johnson herself once showed me a little print of Dartmouth harbour, and told me it was supposed that in old times an iron chain was stretched from rock to rock across its mouth as a means of defence. And that afternoon Fred told

　　　　　Juliana Horatia Ewing

me a splendid story about the chain, and how it was made of silver, and that each link was worth twenty pounds, and how at the end where it was fastened with a padlock every night at sunset, to keep out the French, a lion sat on the ledge of rock at the harbour's mouth, with the key tied round his neck by a sea-green ribbon. He had to have a new ribbon on the first Sunday in every month, Fred said, because his mane dirtied them so fast. A story which Fred had of his grandfather's single-handed encounter with this lion on one occasion, when the gallant captain would let a brig in distress into the harbour after sunset, and the lion would not let him have the key, raised my opinion of his courage and his humanity to the highest point. But what he did at home was nothing to the exploits which Fred recounted of him in foreign lands.

I fancy Fred must have read some real accounts of South America, the tropical forests, the wonderful birds and flowers, and the ruins of those buried cities which have no history; and that on these real marvels he built up his own romances of the Great Stone City, where the captain encountered an awful race of giants with no legs, who carved stones into ornaments with clasp-knives, as the Swiss cut out pretty things in wood, and cracked the cocoa-nuts with their fingers. I am sure he invented flowers as he went along when he was telling me about the forests. He used to look round the garden (which would have satisfied any one who had not seen or heard of what the captain had come across) and say in his slow way, "The blue chalice flower was about the shape of that magnolia, only twice as big, and just the colour of the gentians in the border, and it had a great white tassel hanging out like the cactus in the parlour window, and all the leaves were yellow underneath; and it smelt like rosemary."

If the captain's experiences in other countries outshone what had befallen him in his native land, both these paled before the wonders he had seen, and the emergencies he had been placed in at sea. Fred told me that his grandfather had a diving-bell of his own on board his own ship, and the things he saw when he went down in it must have made his remembrances of the South American forests appear tame by comparison.

Once, in the middle of the Pacific, the captain dropped down in his bell into the midst of a society of sea people who had no hair, but the backs of their heads were shaped like sou'-wester hats. The front rim formed one eyebrow for both eyes, and they could move the peak behind as beavers move their tails, and it helped them to go up and down in the water. They were not exactly mermaids, Fred said, they had no particular tail, it all ended in a kind of fringe of seaweed, which swept after them when they moved, like the train of a lady's dress. The captain was so delighted with them that he stayed below much longer than usual; but in an unlucky moment some of the sea people let the water into the diving-bell, and the captain was nearly drowned. He did become senseless, but when his body floated, it was picked up and restored to life by the first mate, who had been cruising, with tears in his eyes, over the spot in the ship's boat for seven days without taking anything to eat.—"*He* was a Dartmouth man, too," said Fred Johnson.

"He evidently knew what to do in the emergency of drowning," thought I.

I feel as if any one who hears of Fred's stories must think he was a liar. But he really was not. Mr. Johnson was very strict with the boys in some ways, though he was so good-natured, and Fred had been taught to think a lie to get himself out of a scrape or anything of that sort quite as wrong as we should have thought it. But he liked *telling* things. I believe he made them up and amused himself with them in his own head if he had no one to listen. He used to say, "Come and sit in the kitchen garden this afternoon, and I'll *tell* you." And whether he meant me to think them true or not, I certainly did believe in his stories.

One thing always struck me as very odd about Fred Johnson. He was very fond of fruit, and when we sat on the wall and ate the white currants with pounded sugar in a mug between us, I believe he always ate more than I did, though he was "telling" all the time, and I had nothing to do but to listen and eat.

He certainly talked very slowly, in a dreary, monotonous sort of voice, which suited his dull, pasty face better than it suited the subject of his exciting narratives. But I think it seemed to make one all the more impatient to hear what was coming. A very favourite place of ours for "telling" was the wharf (Johnson's wharf, as it was called), where the canal boats came and went, and loaded and unloaded. We made a "coastguard station" among some old timber in the corner, and here we used to sit and watch for the boats.

When a real barge came we generally went over it, for the men knew Fred, and were very good-natured. The barges seemed more like ships than the canal boats did. They had masts, and could sail when they got into the river. Sometimes we went down into the cabin, and peeped into the little berths with sliding shutter fronts, and the lockers, which were like a fixed seat running round two sides of the cabin, with lids opening and showing places to put away things in. I was not famous in the nursery for keeping my things very tidy, but I fancied I could stow my clothes away to perfection in a locker, and almost cook my own dinner with the bargeman's little stove.

And every time a barge was loaded up, and the bargemaster

took his post at the rudder, whilst the old horse strained himself to start—and when the heavy boat swung slowly down the canal and passed out of sight, I felt more and more sorry to be left behind upon the wharf.

CHAPTER VI

S. PHILIP AND S. JAMES—THE MONKEY-BARGE AND THE DOG—WAR, PLAGUE, AND FIRE— THE DULNESS OF EVERYDAY LIFE

There were two churches in our town. Not that the town was so very large or the churches so very small as to make this needful. On the contrary, the town was of modest size, with no traces of having ever been much bigger, and the churches were very large and very handsome. That is, they were fine outside, and might have been very imposing within but for the painted galleries which blocked up the arches above and the tall pews which dwarfed the majestic rows of pillars below. They were not more than a quarter of a mile apart. One was dedicated to S. Philip and the other to S. James, and they were commonly called "the brother churches." In the tower of each hung a peal of eight bells.

One clergyman served both the brother churches, and the services were at S. Philip one week and at S. James the next. We were so accustomed to this that it never struck us as odd. What did seem odd, and perhaps a little dull, was that people in other places should have to go to the same church week after week.

There was only one day in the year on which both the peals

of bells were heard, the Feast of SS. Philip and James, which is also May Day. Then there was morning prayer at S. Philip and evening prayer at S. James, and the bells rang changes and cannons, and went on ringing by turns all the evening, the bell-ringers being escorted from one church to another with May garlands and a sort of triumphal procession. The churches were decorated, and flags put out on the towers, and everybody in the congregation was expected to carry a nosegay.

Rupert and I and Henrietta and Baby Cecil and the servants always enjoyed this thoroughly, and thought the churches delightfully sweet; but my Mother said the smell of the cottage nosegays and the noise of the bells made her feel very ill, which was a pity.

Fred Johnson once told me some wonderful stories about the brother churches. We had gone over the canal to a field not far from the cricketing field, but it was a sort of water-meadow, and lower down, and opposite to the churches, which made us think of them. We had gone there partly to get yellow flags to try and grow them in tubs as Johnson's father did water-lilies, and partly to watch for a canal-boat or "monkey-barge," which was expected up with coal. Fred knew the old man, and we hoped to go home as part of the cargo if the old man's dog would let us; but he was a rough terrier, with an exaggerated conscience, and strongly objected to anything coming on board the boat which was not in the bill of lading. He could not even reconcile himself to the fact that people not connected with barges took the liberty of walking on the canal banks.

"He've been a-going up and down with me these fifteen year," said the old man, "and he barks at 'em still." He barked so fiercely at us that Fred would not go on board, to my great annoyance, for I never feel afraid of dogs, and was quite sure

I could see a disposition to wag about the stumpy tail of the terrier in spite of his "bowfs."

I may have been wrong, but once or twice I fancied that Fred shirked adventures which seemed nothing to me; and I felt this to be very odd, because I am not as brave as I should like to be, and Fred is grandson to the navy captain.

I think Fred wanted to make me forget the canal-boat, which I followed with regretful eyes, for he began talking about the churches.

"It must be splendid to hear all sixteen bells going at once," said he.

"They never do," said I, unmollified.

"They do—*sometimes*," said Fred slowly, and so impressively that I was constrained to ask "When?"

"In great emergencies," was Fred's reply, which startled me. But we had only lived in the place for part of our lives, and Fred's family belonged to it, so he must know better than I.

"Is it to call the doctor?" I asked, thinking of drowning, and broken bones, and apoplectic fits.

"It's to call everybody," said Fred; "that is in time of war, when the town is in danger. And when the Great Plague was here, S. Philip and S. James both tolled all day long with their bells muffled. But when there's a fire they ring backwards, as witches say prayers, you know."

War and the plague had not been here for a very long time, and there had been no fire in the town in my remembrance; but Fred said that awful calamities of the kind had happened within the memory of man, when the town was still built in great part of wood, and that one night, during a high gale, the whole place, except a few houses, had been destroyed by fire. After this the streets were rebuilt of stone and bricks.

These new tales which Fred told me, of places I knew, had a terrible interest peculiarly their own. For the captain's dangers were over for good now, but war, plague, and fire in the town might come again.

I thought of them by day, and dreamed of them by night. Once I remember being awakened, as I fancied, by the clanging of the two peals in discordant unison, and as I opened my eyes a bright light on the wall convinced me that the town was on fire. Fred's vivid descriptions rushed to my mind, and I looked out expecting to see S. Philip and S. James standing up like dark rocks in a sea of dancing flames, their bells ringing backwards, "as witches say prayers." It was only when I saw both the towers standing grey and quiet above the grey and quiet town, and when I found that the light upon the wall came from the street lamp below, that my head seemed to grow clearer, and I knew that no bells were ringing, and that those I fancied I heard were only the prolonged echoes of a bad dream.

I was very glad that it was so, and I did not exactly wish for war or the plague to come back; and yet the more I heard of Fred's tales the more restless I grew, because the days were so dull, and because we never went anywhere, and nothing ever happened.

CHAPTER VII

WE RESOLVE TO RUN AWAY—SCRUPLES—
BABY CECIL—I PREPARE—I RUN AWAY

I think it was Fred's telling me tales of the navy captain's boyhood which put it into our heads that the only way for people at our age, and in our position, to begin a life of adventure is to run away.

The captain had run away. He ran away from school. But then the school was one which it made your hair stand on end to hear of. The master must have been a monster of tyranny, the boys little prodigies of wickedness and misery, and the food such as would have been rejected by respectably reared pigs.

It put his grandson and me at a disadvantage that we had no excuses of the kind for running away from the grammar school. Dr. Jessop was a little pompous, but he was sometimes positively kind. There was not even a cruel usher. I was no dunce, nor was Fred-though he was below me in class—so that we had not even a grievance in connection with our lessons. This made me feel as if there would be something mean and almost dishonourable in running away from school. "I think it would not be fair to the Doctor," said I; "it would look as if he had driven us to it, and he hasn't.

We had better wait till the holidays."

Fred seemed more willing to wait than I had expected; but he planned what we were to do when we did go as vigorously as ever.

It was not without qualms that I thought of running away from home. My mother would certainly be greatly alarmed; but then she was greatly alarmed by so many things to which she afterwards became reconciled! My conscience reproached me more about Rupert and Henrietta. Not one of us had longed for "events" and exploits so earnestly as my sister; and who but Rupert had prepared me for emergencies, not perhaps such as the captain had had to cope with, but of the kinds recognized by the yellow leather book? We had been very happy together—Rupert, Henrietta, Baby Cecil, and I—and we had felt in common the one defect of our lives that there were no events in them; and now I was going to begin a life of adventure, to run away and seek my fortune, without even telling them what I was going to do.

On the other hand, that old mean twinge of jealousy was one of my strongest impulses to adventure-seeking, and it urged me to perform my exploits alone. Some people seem to like dangers and adventures whilst the dangers are going on; Henrietta always seemed to think that the pleasantest part; but I confess that I think one of the best parts must be when they are over and you are enjoying the credit of them. When the captain's adventures stirred me most I looked forward with a thrill of anticipation to my return home—modest from a justifiable pride in my achievements, and so covered with renown by my deeds of daring that I should play second fiddle in the family no more, and that Rupert and Henrietta would outbid each other for my "particular" friendship, and Baby Cecil dog my heels to hear the stories of my adventures.

The thought of Baby Cecil was the heaviest pang I felt when I was dissatisfied with the idea of running away from home. Baby Cecil was the pet of the house. He had been born after my father's death, and from the day he was born everybody conspired to make much of him. Dandy, the Scotch terrier, would renounce a romping ramble with us to keep watch over Baby Cecil when he was really a baby, and was only carried for a dull airing in the nursemaid's arms. I can quite understand Dandy's feelings; for if when one was just preparing for a paperchase, or anything of that sort, Baby Cecil trotted up and, flinging himself head first into one's arms, after his usual fashion, cried, "Baby Cecil 'ants Charlie to tell him a long, long story—*so much!*" it always ended in one's giving up the race or the scramble, and devoting one's self as sedately as Dandy to his service. But I consoled myself with the thought of how Baby Cecil would delight in me, and what stories I should be able to tell him on my return.

The worst of running away now-a-days is that railways and telegrams run faster. I was prepared for any emergency except that of being found and brought home again.

Thinking of this brought to my mind one of Fred's tales of the captain, about how he was pursued by bloodhounds and escaped by getting into water. Water not only retains no scent, it keeps no track. I think perhaps this is one reason why boys so often go to sea when they run away, that no one may be able to follow them. It helped my decision that we would go to sea when we ran away, Fred and I. Besides, there was no other road to strange countries, and no other way of seeing the sea people with the sou'-wester heads.

Fred did not seem to have any scruples about leaving his home, which made me feel how much braver he must be than I. But his head was so full of the plans he made for us, and the lists he drew up of natural products of the earth in various places on which we could live without paying for our living, that he neglected his school-work, and got into scrapes about it. This distressed me very much, for I was working my very best that half on purpose that no one might say that we ran away from our lessons, but that it might be understood that we had gone solely in search of adventure, like sea-captains or any other grown-up travellers.

All Fred's tales now began with the word "suppose." They were not stories of what had happened to his grandfather, but of what might happen to us. The half-holiday that Mr. Johnson's hay was carted we sat behind the farthest haycock all the afternoon with an old atlas on our knees, and Fred "supposed" till my brain whirled to think of all that was coming on us. "Suppose we get on board a vessel bound for Singapore, and hide behind some old casks—" he would say, coasting strange continents with his stumpy little forefinger, as recklessly as the captain himself; on which of course I asked, "What is Singapore like?" which enabled Fred to close the atlas and lie back among the hay and say whatever he could think of and I could believe.

Meanwhile we saved up our pocket-money and put it in a canvas bag, as being sailor-like. Most of the money was Fred's, but he was very generous about this, and said I was to take care of it as I was more managing than he. And we practised tree-climbing to be ready for the masts, and ate earth-nuts to learn to live upon roots in case we were thrown upon a desert island. Of course we did not give up our proper meals, as we were not obliged to yet, and I sometimes felt rather doubtful about how we should feel living upon nothing but roots for breakfast, dinner, and tea. However, I had observed that whenever the captain was wrecked a barrel of biscuits went ashore soon afterwards, and I hoped it might always be so in wrecks, for biscuits go a long way, especially sailors' biscuits, which are large.

I made a kind of handbook for adventure-seekers, too, in an old exercise book, showing what might be expected and should be prepared for in a career like the captain's. I divided it under certain heads: Hardships, Dangers, Emergencies, Wonders, &c. These were subdivided again thus: Hardships— I, Hunger; 2, Thirst; 3, Cold; 4, Heat; 5, No Clothes; and so forth. I got all my information from Fred, and I read my lists over and over again to get used to the ideas, and to feel brave. And on the last page I printed in red ink the word "Glory."

And so the half went by and came to an end; and when the old Doctor gave me my three prizes, and spoke of what he hoped I would do next half, my blushes were not solely from modest pride.

The first step of our runaway travels had been decided upon long ago. We were to go by barge to London. "And from London you can go anywhere," Fred said.

The day after the holidays began I saw a canal-boat lading at the wharf, and finding she was bound for London I told Fred of it. But he said we had better wait for a barge, and that there would be one on Thursday. "Or if you don't think you can be ready by then, we can wait for the next," he added. He seemed quite willing to wait, but (remembering that the captain's preparations for his longest voyage had only taken him eighteen and a half minutes by the chronometer, which was afterwards damaged in the diving-bell accident, and which I had seen with my own eyes, in confirmation of the story) I said I should be ready any time at half-an-hour's notice, and Thursday was fixed as the day of our departure.

To facilitate matters it was decided that Fred should invite me to spend Wednesday with him, and to stay all night, for the barge was to start at half-past six o'clock on Thursday morning.

I was very busy on Wednesday. I wrote a letter to my mother in which I hoped I made it quite clear that ambition and not discontent was leading me to run away. I also made a will, dividing my things fairly between Rupert, Henrietta, and Baby Cecil, in case I should be drowned at sea. My knife, my prayer-book, the ball of string belonging to my kite, and my little tool-box I took away with me. I also took the match-box from the writing-table, but I told Mother of it in the letter. The captain used to light his fires by rubbing sticks together, but I had tried it, and thought matches would be much better, at any rate to begin with.

Rupert was lying under the crab-tree, and Henrietta was reading to him, when I went away. Rupert was getting much stronger; he could walk with a stick, and was going back to school next half. I felt a very unreasonable vexation because they seemed quite cheerful. But as I was leaving the garden to go over the fields, Baby Cecil came running after me, with his wooden spade in one hand and a plant of chick weed in the other, crying: "Charlie, dear! Come and tell Baby Cecil a story." I kissed him, and tied his hat on, which had come off as he ran.

"Not now, Baby," I said; "I am going out now, and you are gardening."

"I don't want to garden," he pleaded. "Where are you going? Take me with you."

"I am going to Fred Johnson's," I said bravely.

Baby Cecil was a very good child, though he was so much petted. He gave a sigh of disappointment, but only said very gravely, "Will you promise, *onyer-onner*, to tell me one when you come back?"

"I promise to tell you lots *when I come back*, on my honour," was my answer.

I had to skirt the garden-hedge for a yard or two before turning off across the meadow. In a few minutes I heard a voice on the other side. Baby Cecil had run down the inside, and was poking his face through a hole, and kissing both hands to me. There came into my head a wonder whether his face would be much changed next time I saw it. I little guessed when and how that would be. But when he cried, "Come back *very soon*, Charlie dear," my imperfect valour utterly gave way, and hanging my head I ran, with hot tears pouring over my face, all the way to Johnson's wharf.

When Fred saw my face he offered to give up the idea if I felt faint-hearted about it. Nothing that he could have said would have dried my tears so soon. Every spark of pride in me blazed up to reject the thought of turning craven now. Besides, I longed for a life of adventure most sincerely; and I was soon quite happy again in the excitement of being so near to what I had longed for.

CHAPTER VIII

WE GO ON BOARD—THE PIE—AN EXPLOSION— MR. ROWE THE BARGE-MASTER—THE 'WHITE LION'—TWO LETTERS—WE DOUBT MR. ROWE'S GOOD FAITH

The dew was still heavy on the grass when Fred and I crossed the drying-ground about five o'clock on Thursday morning, and scrambled through a hedge into our "coastguard" corner on the wharf. We did not want to be seen by the barge-master till we were too far from home to be put ashore.

The freshness of early morning in summer has some quality which seems to go straight to the heart. I felt intensely happy. There lay the barge, the sun shining on the clean deck, and from the dewy edges of the old ropes, and from the barge-master's zinc basin and pail put out to sweeten in the air.

"She won't leave us behind this time!" I cried, turning triumphantly to Fred.

"Take care of the pie," said Fred.

It was a meat-pie which he had taken from the larder this

morning; but he had told Mrs. Johnson about it in the letter he had left behind him; and had explained that we took it instead of the breakfast we should otherwise have eaten. We felt that earth-nuts might not be forthcoming on the canal banks, or even on the wharf at Nine Elms when we reached London.

At about a quarter to six Johnson's wharf was quite deserted. The barge-master was having breakfast ashore, and the second man had gone to the stable. "We had better hide ourselves now," I said. So we crept out and went on board. We had chosen our hiding-place before. Not in the cabin, of course, nor among the cargo, where something extra thrown in at the last moment might smother us if it did not lead to our discovery, but in the fore part of the boat, in a sort of well or *hold*, where odd things belonging to the barge itself were stowed away, and made sheltered nooks into which we could creep out of sight. Here we found a very convenient corner, and squatted down, with the pie at our feet, behind a hamper, a box, a coil of rope, a sack of hay, and a very large ball, crossed four ways with rope, and with a rope-tail, which puzzled me extremely.

"It's like a giant tadpole," I whispered to Fred.

"Don't nudge me," said Fred. "My pockets are full, and it hurts."

My pockets were far from light. The money-bag was heavily laden with change—small in value but large in coin. The box of matches was with it and the knife. String, nails, my prayer-book, a pencil, some writing-paper, the handbook, and a more useful hammer than the one in my tool-box filled another pocket. Some gooseberries and a piece of cake were in my trousers, and I carried the tool-box in my hands. We each had a change of linen, tied up in a pocket-handkerchief.

Fred would allow of nothing else. He said that when our jackets and trousers were worn out we must make new clothes out of an old sail.

Waiting is very dull work. After awhile, however, we heard voices, and the tramp of the horse, and then the barge-master and Mr. Johnson's foreman and other men kept coming and going on deck, and for a quarter of an hour we had as many hairbreadth escapes of discovery as the captain himself could have had in the circumstances. At last somebody threw the barge-master a bag of something (fortunately soft) which he was leaving behind, and which he chucked on to the top of my head. Then the driver called to his horse, and the barge gave a jerk, which threw Fred on to the pie, and in a moment more we were gliding slowly and smoothly down the stream.

When we were fairly off we ventured to peep out a little, and stretch our cramped limbs. There was no one on board but the barge-master, and he was at the other end of the vessel, smoking and minding his rudder. The driver was walking on the towing-path by the old grey horse. The motion of the boat was so smooth that we seemed to be lying still whilst villages and orchards and green banks and osier-beds went slowly by, as though the world were coming to show itself to us, instead of our going out to see the world.

When we passed the town we felt some anxiety for fear we should be stopped; but there was no one on the bank, and though the towers of S. Philip and S. James appeared again and again in lessening size as we looked back, there came at last a bend in the canal, when a high bank of gorse shut out the distance, and we saw them no more.

In about an hour, having had no breakfast, we began to speak seriously of the pie. (I had observed Fred breaking little corners from the crust with an absent air more than once.)

Thinking of the first subdivision under the word Hardships in my handbook, I said, "I'm afraid we ought to wait till we are *worse hungry.*"

But Fred said, "Oh no!" And that out adventure-seeking it was quite impossible to save and plan and divide your meals exactly, as you could never tell what might turn up. The captain always said, "Take good luck and bad luck and pot-luck as they come!" So Fred assured me, and we resolved to abide by the captain's rule.

"We may have to weigh out our food with a bullet, like Admiral Bligh, next week," said Fred.

"So we may," said I. And the thought must have given an extra relish to the beefsteak and hard-boiled eggs, for I never tasted anything so good.

Whether the smell of the pie went aft, or whether something else made the barge-master turn round and come forward, I do not know; but when we were encumbered with open clasp-knives, and full mouths, we saw him bearing down upon us, and in a hasty movement of retreat I lost my balance, and went backward with a crash upon a tub of potatoes.

The noise this made was not the worst part of the business. I was tightly wedged amongst the odds and ends, and the money-bag being sharply crushed against the match-box, which was by this time well warmed, the matches exploded in a body, and whilst I was putting as heroic a face as I could on the pain I was enduring in my right funny-bone, Fred cried, "Your jacket's smoking. You're on fire!"

Whether Mr. Rowe, the barge-master, had learnt presence of mind out of a book, I do not know; but before Fred and I could even think of what to do in the emergency, my jacket was off, the matches were overboard, and Mr. Rowe was squeezing the smouldering fire out of my pocket, rather more deliberately than most men brush their hats. Then, after civilly holding the jacket for me to put it on again, he took off his hat, took his handkerchief out of it, and wiped his head, and replacing both, with his eyes upon us, said, more deliberately still, "Well, young gentlemen, this is a nice start!"

It was impossible to resist the feeling of confidence inspired by Mr. Rowe's manner, his shrewd and stolid appearance, and his promptness in an emergency. Besides, we were completely at his mercy. We appealed to it, and told him our plans. We offered him a share of the pie too, which he accepted with conscious condescension. When the dish was empty he brought his handkerchief into use once more, and then said, in a peculiarly oracular manner, "You just look to me, young gentlemen, and I'll put you in the way of every think."

The immediate advantage we took of this offer was to ask about whatever interested us in the landscape constantly passing before our eyes, or the barge-furniture at our feet. The cord-compressed balls were shore-fenders, said Mr. Rowe, and were popped over the side when the barge was likely to grate against the shore, or against another vessel.

"Them's osier-beds. They cuts 'em every year or so for basket-work. Wot's that little bird a-hanging head downwards? It's a titmouse looking for insects, that is. There's scores on 'em in the osier-beds. Aye, aye, the yellow lilies is pretty enough, but there's a lake the other way—a mile or two beyond your father's, Master Fred—where there's white water-lilies. They're pretty, if you like! It's a rum thing in spring," continued Mr. Rowe, between puffs of his pipe, "to see them lilies come up from the bottom of the canal; the leaves packed

Juliana Horatia Ewing

as neat as any parcel, and when they git to the top, they turns down and spreads out on the water as flat as you could spread a cloth upon a table."

As a rule, Mr. Rowe could give us no names for the aquatic plants at which we clutched as we went by, nor for the shells we got out of the mud; but his eye for a water-rat was like a terrier's. It was the only thing which seemed to excite him.

About mid-day we stopped by a village, where Mr. Rowe had business. The horse was to rest and bait here; and the barge-master told us that if we had "a shilling or so about" us, we might dine on excellent bread and cheese at the *White Lion*, or even go so far as poached eggs and yet more excellent bacon, if our resources allowed of it. We were not sorry to go ashore. There was absolutely no shelter on the deck of the barge from the sunshine, which was glaringly reflected by the water. The inn parlour was low, but it was dark and cool. I felt doubtful about the luxury even of cheese after that beefsteak-pie but Fred smacked his lips and ordered eggs and bacon, and I paid for them out of the canvas-bag.

As we sat together I said, "I wrote a letter to my mother, Fred. Did you write to Mrs. Johnson?"

Fred nodded, and pulled a scrap of dirty paper from his pocket, saying, "That's the letter; but I made a tidy copy of it afterwards."

I have said that Fred was below me in class, though he is older; and he was very bad at spelling. Otherwise the letter did very well, except for smudges.

"DEAR MOTHER,

"Charlie and I are going to run away at least by the time you get this we have run away but never mind for wen weve seen the wurld were cumming back we took the pi wich I hope you wont mind as we had no brekfust and I'll bring back the dish we send our best love and I've no more to tell you to-day from your affectionate son FRED."

I saw Mr. Rowe myself very busy in the bar of the *White Lion*, with a sheet of paper and an old steel pen, which looked as if the point had been attenuated to that hair-like fineness by sheer age. He started at the sight of me, which caused him to drop a very large blot of ink from the very sharp point of the pen on to his paper. I left him wiping it up with his handkerchief. But it never struck me that he was writing a letter on the same subject as Fred and I had been writing about. He was, however: and Mr. Johnson keeps it tied up with Fred's to this day. The spelling was of about the same order.

"MR. JOHNSON. HONERD SIR.

"i rites in duty bound to acqaint you that the young genlemen is with me, looking out for Advenchurs and asking your pardon i wish they may find them as innercent as 2 Babes in the Wood on the London and Lancingford Canal were they come aboard quite unknown to me and blowed theirselves up with lucifers the fust go off and you've no need to trubble yourself sir ill keep my I on them and bring em safe to hand with return cargo and hoping you'll excuse the stamp not expecting to have to rite from the fust stoppige your obedient humble servant

"SAMUEL ROWE."

As I have said, we did not suspect that Mr. Rowe had

betrayed us by post; but in the course of the afternoon Fred said to me, "I'll tell you what, Charlie, I know old Rowe well, and he's up to any trick, and sure to want to keep in with my father. If we don't take care he'll take us back with him. And what fools we shall look then!"

The idea was intolerable; but I warned Fred to carefully avoid betraying that we suspected him. The captain had had worse enemies to outwit, and had kept a pirate in good humour for a much longer voyage by affability and rum. We had no means of clouding Mr. Rowe's particularly sharp wits with grog, but we resolved to be amiable and wary, and when we did get to London to look out for the first opportunity of giving the barge-master the slip.

CHAPTER IX

A COASTING VOYAGE—MUSK ISLAND—
LINNET FLASH—MR. ROWE AN OLD TAR—
THE DOG-FANCIER AT HOME

It was a delightful feature of our first voyage—and one which we could not hope to enjoy so often in voyages to come—that we were always close to land, and this on both sides. We could touch either coast without difficulty, and as the barge stopped several times during the day to rest the horse, Fred and I had more than one chance of going ashore.

I hope to have many a voyage yet, and to see stranger people and places than I saw then, but I hardly hope ever to enjoy myself so much again. I have long ago found out that Fred's stories of the captain's adventures were not true stories, and as I have read and learned more about the world than I knew at that time, I know now that there are only certain things which one can meet with by land or by sea. But when Fred and I made our first voyage in emulation of his grandfather there was no limit to my expectations, or to what we were prepared to see or experience at every fresh bend of the London and Lancingford Canal.

I remember one of Fred's stories about the captain was of his spending a year and a day on an island called Musk Island, in the Pacific. He had left the ship, Fred said, to do a little exploring alone in his gig. Not knowing at that time that the captain's gig is a boat, I was a good deal puzzled, I remember, to think of Mrs. Johnson's red-faced father crossing the sea in a gig like the one Mr. Bustard used to go his professional "rounds" in. And when Fred spoke of his "pulling himself" I was yet more bewildered by the unavoidable conclusion that they had no horse on board, and that the gallant and ever-ready captain went himself between the shafts. The wonder of his getting to Musk Island in that fashion was, however, eclipsed by the wonders he found when he did get there. Musk-hedges and bowers ten feet high, with flowers as large as bindweed blossoms, and ladies with pale gold hair all dressed in straw-coloured satin, and with such lovely faces that the captain vowed that no power on earth should move him till he had learned enough of the language to propose the health of the Musk Island beauties in a suitable speech after dinner. "And there he would have lived and died, I believe," Fred would say, "if that first mate, who saved his life before, had not rescued him by main force, and taken him back to his ship."

I am reminded of this story when I think of the island in Linnet Lake, for we were so deeply charmed by it that we very nearly broke our voyage, as the captain broke his, to settle on it.

Mr. Rowe called the lake Linnet Flash. Wherever the canal seemed to spread out, and then go on again narrow and like a river, the barge-master called these lakes "flashes" of the canal. There is no other flash on that canal so large or so beautiful as Linnet Lake, and in the middle of the lake lies the island.

It was about three o'clock, the hottest part of a summer's day, and Fred and I, rather faint with the heat, were sitting on a coil of rope holding a clean sheet, which Mr. Rowe had brought up from the cabin to protect our heads and backs from sunstroke. We had refused to take shelter below, and sat watching the fields and hedges, which seemed to palpitate in the heat as they went giddily by, and Mr. Rowe, who stood quite steady, conversing coolly with the driver. The driver had been on board for the last hour, the way being clear, and the old horse quite able to take care of itself and us, and he and the barge-master had pocket-handkerchiefs under their hats like the sou'-wester flaps of the captain's sea-friends. Fred had dropped his end of the sheet to fall asleep, and I was protecting us both, when the driver bawled some directions to the horse in their common language, and the barge-master said, "Here's a bit of shade for you, Master Fred;" and we roused up and found ourselves gliding under the lee of an island covered with trees.

"Oh, *do* stop here!" we both cried.

"Well, I don't mind," said Mr. Rowe, removing his hat, and mopping himself with his very useful pocket-handkerchief. "Jem, there's a bit of grass there, let her have a mouthful."

"I thought you'd like this," he continued; "there ain't a prettier bit between here and Pyebridge."

It was so lovely, that the same idea seized both Fred and me: Why not settle here, at least for a time? It was an uninhabited island, only waiting to be claimed by some adventurous navigator, and obviously fertile. The prospect of blackberries on the mainland was particularly fine, and how they would ripen in this blazing sun! Birds sang in the trees above; fish leaping after flies broke the still surface of the water with a musical splash below; and beyond a doubt there must be the largest and the sweetest of earth-nuts on the island, easy to get out of the deep beds of untouched leaf-mould. And when

Mr. Rowe cried "Look!" and we saw a water-fowl scud across the lake, leaving a sharp trail like a line of light behind her, we felt that we might spend all our savings in getting to the Pacific Ocean, and not find when we got there a place which offered more natural resources to the desert islander.

If the barge-master would have gone ashore on the mainland out of the way, and if we could have got ashore on the island without help, we should not have confided our plans to so doubtful a friend. As it was, we were obliged to tell Mr. Rowe that we proposed to found a settlement in Linnet Lake, and he was completely opposed to the idea.

It was only when he said (with that air of reserved and funded knowledge which gave such unfathomable depth to his irony, and made his sayings so oracular)—"There's very different places in the world to Linnet Flash"—that we began to be ashamed of our hasty enthusiasm, and to think that it would be a pity to stop so short in our adventurous career.

So we decided to go on; but the masterly way in which Mr. Rowe spoke of the world made me think he must have seen a good deal of it, and when we had looked our last upon the island, and had crept with lowered mast under an old brick bridge where young ferns hung down from the archway, and when we were once more travelling between flat banks and coppices that gave us no shelter, I said to the barge-master— "Have you ever been at sea, Mr. Rowe?"

"Seven*teen* year in the Royal Navy," said Mr. Rowe, with a strong emphasis upon *teen*, as if he feared we might do him the injustice of thinking he had only served his Queen and country for seven.

For the next two hours Fred and I sat, indifferent alike to the sunshine and the shore, in rapt attention to Mr. Rowe's narrative of his experiences at sea under the flag that has

"Braved a thousand years the battle and the breeze."

I believe Fred enjoyed them simply as stories, but they fanned in my heart that restless fever for which sea-breezes are the only cure. I think Mr. Rowe got excited himself as he recalled old times. And when he began to bawl sea-songs with a voice like an Atlantic gale, and when he vowed in cadence

"A sailor's life is the life for me,"

I felt that it was the life for me also, and expressed myself so strongly to that effect that Mr. Rowe became alarmed for the consequences of his indiscretion, and thenceforward told us sea-stories with the obvious and quite futile intention of disgusting me with what I already looked upon as my profession.

But the barge-master's rapid change of tactics convinced me more and more that we could not safely rely on him to help us in our plans.

About five o'clock he made tea on board, and boiled the water on the little stove in the cabin. I was very anxious to help, and it was I who literally made the tea, whilst Mr. Rowe's steadier hand cut thick slices of bread-and-butter from a large loaf. There was only one cup and saucer. Fred and I shared the cup, and the barge-master took the saucer. By preference, he said, as the tea cooled quicker.

The driver had tea after we returned to the deck and could attend to the horse and boat.

Except the island in Linnet Lake, the most entertaining events of the first day of our voyage were our passing villages or detached houses on the canal banks.

Of the latter by far the most interesting was that of a dog-fancier, from whose residence melodious howls, in the dog-dialect of every tribe deserving to be represented in so choice a company, were wafted up the stream, and met our ears before our eyes beheld the landing-stage of the establishment, where the dog-fancier and some of his dogs were lounging in the cool of the evening, and glad to see the barge.

The fancier knew Mr. Rowe, and refreshed him (and us) with shandy-gaff in horn tumblers. Some of the dogs who did not, barked incessantly at us, wagging their tails at the same time, however, as if they had some doubts of the correctness of their judgment in the matter. One very small, very white, and very fluffy toy-dog, with a dove-coloured ribbon, was—no doubt—incurably ill-tempered and inhospitable; but a large brindled bull-dog, trying politely but vainly to hide his teeth and tongue, wagged what the fancier had left him of a tail, and dribbled with the pleasure of making our acquaintance, after the wont of his benevolent and much-maligned family. I have since felt pretty certain that Mr. Rowe gave his friend a sketch of our prospects and intentions in the same spirit in which he had written to Mr. Johnson, and I distinctly overheard the dog-fancier make some reply, in which the words "hoffer a reward" were audible. But the barge-master shook his head at suggestions probably drawn from his friend's professional traditions, though the fancier told him some very good story about the ill-tempered toy-dog, to which he referred with such violent jerks of the head as threatened to throw his fur cap on to that of the brindled gentleman who sat dripping and smiling at his feet.

When Mr. Rowe began to tell him something good in return, and in spite of my utmost endeavours not to hear anything, the words "Linnet Flash" became audible, I blushed to hear the fancier choking over his shandy-gaff with laughter, and I feared at our project for settling on the island.

The interview was now at an end, but as Mr. Rowe stepped briskly on board, the fur cap nodded to the forehatch, where Fred and I were sitting on coiled ropes, and the fancier said very knowingly, "The better the breed the gamier the beast."

He patted the bull-dog as he said it, and the bull-dog kissed his dirty hand.

"Hup to hanythink," were Mr. Rowe's parting words, as he went aft, and the driver called to his horse.

He may have referred to the bull-dog, but I had some doubts about it, even then.

CHAPTER X

LOCKS—WE THINK OF GOING ON THE TRAMP—
PYEBRIDGE—WE SET SAIL

During our first day's voyage we passed two locks. There was one not very far from home, and Fred and I had more than once been to see a barge pass it, sitting on the bank whilst the boat gradually sank to the level of the water below.

It was great fun being on board whilst the barge went down and down, though I must say we did not feel anything peculiar, we sank so gradually.

"Just fancy if it was a hole in the ship's bottom," said Fred, "and we were settling down with all on board. Some ships do, and are never heard of again."

We amused ourselves as we went along by guessing beforehand on which shore the next house or hamlet would appear. We betted shillings on the result, but neither of us won or lost, for however often the shillings changed hands, they remained in the canvas bag.

Perhaps places look more as if events happened in them if you do not if now them well. I noticed that even our town looked more interesting from the water than I had ever seen it look, so I dare say to strangers it does not appear so dull as it is. All the villages on the canal banks looked interesting. We passed one soon after tea, where the horse rested under some old willows by the towing-path, and we and Mr. Rowe went ashore. Whilst the barge-master delivered a parcel to a friend, Fred and I strolled into a lane which led us past cottages with very gay gardens to the church. The church was not at all like S. Philip or S. James. It was squat, and ivy-covered, and carefully restored; and it stood in a garden where the flowers almost hid the graves. Just outside the lych-gate, four lanes met, and all of them were so shady and inviting, and it was so impossible to say what they might not lead to, that I said to Fred,

"You said the only way to run away besides going to sea was to *tramp*. It sounds rather low, but we needn't beg, and I think walking would be nice for a change, and I don't believe it would be much slower than the barge, and it would be so much shadier. And we could get off from Old Rowe at once, and hide if we heard anybody coming. I wonder how far it is to London now?"

"Not far, I dare say," said Fred, who was pleased by the idea; "and if we keep on we must get there in time. And we can get things to eat in the hedges, which we can't do on the barge."

At this moment there passed a boy, to whom I said, "Which is the way to London, if you please?" for there were four roads to choose from.

"What d' say?" said the boy.

I repeated my question.

Juliana Horatia Ewing

"Dunno," he replied, trying to cram half his hand into his mouth. The captain would have thought him very stupid if he had met him as a native in one of the islands of the Pacific, I am sure; but I followed him, and begged him to try and think if he had not heard of people going to London.

At last his face brightened. He was looking over my head down the lane. "There's a man a-cummin yonder's always a-going to Lunnon," said he. Visions of a companion on our tramp—also perhaps in search of adventures—made me look briskly round. "Him with the pipe, as b'longs to the barge," the boy exclaimed.

It was indeed Mr. Rowe come to look for us, and we had to try and seem glad to see him, and to go on board once more.

Towards evening the canal banks became dotted with fishers of all ages and degrees, fishing very patiently, though they did not seem to catch much.

Soon after dark we reached the town of Pyebridge.

When the barge lay-to for the night, and the driver was taking the horse away to the stable, Mr. Rowe confronted us, in his firmest manner, with the question, "And where are you going to sleep, young gentlemen?"

"Where are *you* going to sleep, Mr. Rowe?" said I, after a thoughtful pause.

"*I* sleeps below, but the captain's cabin is guv up to no one— unless it be the Queen," replied the barge-master, humorously but decidedly.

"We should like to sleep on deck," said I.

But Mr. Rowe would not hear of it, on account of various dreadful diseases which he assured us would be contracted by sleeping "in the damps of the water," "the dews of the *h*air," and "the rays of the moon."

"There's a hotel—" he began; but I said at once, "We couldn't afford a hotel, but if you know of any very cheap place we should be much obliged."

Mr. Rowe took off his hat and took out his handkerchief, though it was no longer hot. Having cleared his brain, he said he "would see," and he finally led us along one of the pebbled streets of Pyebridge to a small house with a small shop-window for the sale of vegetables, and with a card announcing that there were beds to let. A very little old woman got up from behind a very big old geranium in the window as we entered, and with her Mr. Rowe made our arrangements for the night. We got a clean bed, and had a mug of milk and a slice of bread and treacle apiece for breakfast the next morning, and I paid two shillings. As I thanked the old lady and bade her good day, she called to me to hold out my hat, which she filled with cherries, and then stood at the door and watched us out of sight.

There was a railway station in Pyebridge, and we might easily have escaped from Mr. Rowe, and gone by train to London. But besides the fact that our funds were becoming low, the water had a new attraction for us. We had left the canal behind, and were henceforward on a river. If the wind favoured us we were to sail.

"A canal's nothing to a river," said Mr. Rowe, "same as a river's nothing to the sea," and when Fred had some difficulty in keeping his hat on in the gusty street (mine was in use as a fruit-basket), and the barge-master said it was a "nice fresh morning," I felt that life on Linnet Island would have been tame indeed compared to the hopes and fears of a career which depended on the winds and waves.

And when the boom went up the barge's mast, and the tightly corded roll of dark canvas began to struggle for liberty, and writhe and flap with throttling noises above our heads, and when Mr. Rowe wrestled with it and the driver helped him, and Fred and I tried to, and were all but swept overboard in consequence, whilst the barge-master encouraged himself by strange and savage sounds—and when the sunshine caught our nut-brown sail just as she spread gallantly to the breeze, our excitement grew till we both cried in one breath,

"This is something *like* being at sea!"

CHAPTER XI

MR. ROWE ON BARGE-WOMEN—THE RIVER— NINE ELMS—A MYSTERIOUS NOISE—ROUGH QUARTERS—A CHEAP SUPPER—JOHN'S BERTH— WE MAKE OUR ESCAPE—OUT INTO THE WORLD

Mr. Rowe is quite right. A canal is nothing to a river.

There was a wide piece of water between us and one of the banks now, and other barges went by us, some sailing, some towing only, and two or three with women at the rudder, and children on the deck.

"I wouldn't have my wife and fam'ly on board for something!" said Mr. Rowe grimly.

"Have you got a family, Mr. Rowe?" I inquired.

"Yes, sir," said the barge-master. "I have, like other folk. But women and children's best ashore."

"Of course they are," said I.

"If you was to turn over in your mind what they *might* be good for now," he continued, with an unfathomable eye on the mistress of a passing canal-boat, "you'd say washing the

Juliana Horatia Ewing

decks and keeping the pots clean. And they don't do it as well as a man—not by half."

"They seem to steer pretty well," said I.

"I've served in very different vessels to what I'm in now," said Mr. Rowe, avoiding a reply, "and I *may* come as low as a monkey-barge and coal; but I'm blessed if ever I see myself walk on the towing-path and leave the missus in command on board."

At this moment a barge came sailing alongside of us.

"Oh look!" cried Fred, "it's got a white horse painted on the sail."

"That's a lime barge, sir," said Mr. Rowe; "all lime barges is marked that way."

She was homeward bound, and empty, and soon passed us, but we went at a pretty good pace ourselves. The wind kept favourable, a matter in which Fred and I took the deepest interest. We licked our fingers, and held them up to see which side got cooled by the breeze, and whenever this experiment convinced me that it was still behind us, I could not help running back to Fred to say with triumph, "The wind's dead aft," as if he knew nothing about it.

At last this seemed to annoy him, so I went to contain myself by sitting on the potato-tub and watching the shore.

We got into the Thames earlier than usual, thanks to the fair wind.

The world is certainly a very beautiful place. I suppose when I get right out into it, and go to sea, and to other countries, I shall think nothing of England and the Thames, but it was all new and wonderful to Fred and me then. The green slopes and fine trees, and the houses with gardens down to the river, and boats rocking by the steps, the osier islands, which Mr. Rowe called "Aits," and the bridges where the mast had to be lowered, all the craft on the water—the red-sailed barges with one man on board—the steamers with crowded decks and gay awnings—the schooners, yachts, and pleasure boats—and all the people on shore, the fishers, and the people with water-dogs and sticks, the ladies with fine dresses and parasols, and the ragged boys who cheered us as we went by—everything we saw and heard delighted us, and the only sore place in my heart was where I longed for Rupert and Henrietta to enjoy it too.

Later on we saw London. It was in the moonlight that we passed Chelsea. Mr. Rowe pointed out the Hospital, in which the pensioners must have been asleep, for not a wooden leg was stirring. In less than half-an-hour afterwards we were at the end of our voyage.

The first thing which struck me about Nine Elms was that they were not to be seen. I had thought of those elms more than once under the burning sun of the first day. I had imagined that we should land at last on some green bank, where the shelter of a majestic grove might tempt Mr. Rowe to sleep, while Fred and I should steal gently away to the neighbouring city, and begin a quite independent search for adventures. But I think I must have mixed up with my expectations a story of one of the captain's escapes—from a savage chief in a mango-grove.

Our journey's end was not quite what I had thought it would be, but it was novel and interesting enough. We seemed to have thoroughly got to the town. Very old houses with feeble lights in their paper-patched windows made strange

Juliana Horatia Ewing

reflections on the river. The pier looked dark and dirty even by moonlight, and threw blacker and stranger shadows still.

Mr. Rowe was busy and tired, and—we thought—a little inclined to be cross.

"I wonder where we shall sleep!" said Fred, looking timidly up at the dark old houses.

I have said before that I find it hard work to be very brave after dark, but I put a good face on the matter, and said I dared say old Rowe would find us a cheap bedroom.

"London's an awful place for robbers and murders, you know," said Fred.

I was hoping the cold shiver running down my back was due to what the barge-master called "the damps from the water"—when a wail like the cry of a hurt child made my skin stiffen into goose-prickles. A wilder moan succeeded, and then one of the windows of one of the dark houses was opened, and something thrown out which fell heavily down. Mr. Rowe was just coming on board again, and I found courage in the emergency to gasp out, "What was that?"

"Wot's wot?" said Mr. Rowe testily.

"That noise and the falling thing."

"Somebody throwing, somethin' at a cat," said the barge-master. "Stand aside, sir, *if* you please."

It was a relief, but when at length Mr. Rowe came up to me with his cap off, in the act of taking out his handkerchief, and said, "I suppose you're no richer than you was yesterday, young gentlemen—how about a bed?"—I said, "No—o. That is, I mean if you can get us a cheap one in a safe—I mean a respectable place."

"If you leaves a comfortable 'ome, sir," moralized the barge-master, "to go a-looking for adventures in this fashion, you must put up with rough quarters, and wot you can get."

"We'll go anywhere you think right, Mr. Rowe," said I diplomatically.

"I knows a waterman," said Mr. Rowe, "that was in the Royal Navy like myself. He lives near here, and they're decent folk. The place is a poor place, but you'll have to make the best of it, young gentlemen, and a shilling 'll cover the damage. If you wants supper you must pay for it. Give the missis the money, and she'll do the best she can, and bring you the change to a half-farthing."

My courage was now fully restored, but Fred was very much overwhelmed by the roughness of the streets we passed through, the drunken, quarrelling, poverty-struck people, and the grim, dirty old houses.

"We shall be out of it directly," I whispered, and indeed in a few minutes more Mr. Rowe turned up a shabby entry, and led us to one of several lower buildings round a small court. The house he stopped at was cleaner within than without, and the woman was very civil.

"It's a very poor place, sir," said she; "but we always keep a berth, as his father calls it, for our son John."

"But we can't take your son's bed," said I; "we'll sit up here, if you will let us."

"Bless ye, love," said the woman, "John's in foreign parts.

He's a sailor, sir, like his father before him; but John's in the merchant service."

Mr. Rowe now bade us good-night. "I'll be round in the morning," said he.

"What o'clock, Mr. Rowe?" I asked; I had a reason for asking.

"There ain't much in the way of return cargo," he replied; "but I've a bit of business to do for your father, Mr. Fred, that'll take me until half-past nine. I'll be here by then, young gentlemen, and show you about a bit."

"It's roughish quarters for you," added the bargemaster, looking round; "but you'll find rougher quarters at sea, Master Charles."

Mr. Howe's moralizings nettled me, and they did no good, for my whole thoughts were now bent on evading his guardianship and getting to sea, but poor Fred was quite overpowered. "I wish we were safe home again," he almost sobbed when I went up to the corner into which he had huddled himself.

"You'll be all right when we're afloat," said I.

"I'm so hungry," he moaned.

I was hungry myself, and decided to order some supper, so when the woman came up and civilly asked if she could do anything for us before we went to bed, I said, "If you please we're rather hungry, but we can't afford anything very expensive. Do you think you can get us anything—rather cheap—for supper?"

"A red herring?" she suggested.

"What price are they?" I felt bound to inquire.

"Mrs. Jones has them beautiful and mild at two for a penny. You *can* get 'em at three a penny, but you wouldn't like 'em, sir."

I felt convinced by the expression of her face that I should not, so I ordered two.

"And a penny loaf?" suggested our landlady, getting her bonnet from behind the door.

"If you please."

"And a bunch of radishes and a pint of fourpenny would be fivepence-half-penny the lot, sir."

"If you please. And, if you please, that will do," said I, drawing a shilling from the bag, for the thought of the herrings made me ravenous, and I wanted her to go. She returned quickly with the bread, and herrings. The "fourpenny" proved to be beer. She gave me sixpence-half-penny in change, which puzzled my calculations.

"You said *fourpenny*," said I, indicating the beer.

"Yes, sir, but it's a pint," was the reply; and it was only when in after-years I learned that beer at fourpence a quart is known to some people as "fourpenny" that I got that part of the reckoning of the canvas bag straight in my own mind.

The room had an unwholesome smell about it, which the odour from our fried herrings soon pleasantly overpowered. The bread was good, and the beer did us no harm. Fred picked up his spirits again; when Mr. Rowe's old mate came home he found us very cheerful and chatty. Fred asked him about the son who was at sea, but I had some more important questions to put, and I managed so to do, and with a sufficiently careless air.

"I suppose there are lots of ships at London?" said I.

"In the Docks, sir, plenty," said our host.

"And where are the Docks?" I inquired. "Are they far from you?"

"Well, you see, sir, there's a many docks. There's the East India Docks, St. Katharine's Docks, and the Commercial Docks, and Victoria Dock, and lots more."

I pondered. Ships in the East India Dock probably went only to India. St. Katharine conveyed nothing to my mind. I did not fancy Commercial Docks. I felt a loyal inclination towards the Victoria Dock.

"How do people get from here to Victoria Dock now, if they want to?" I asked.

"Well, of course, sir, you can go down the river, or part that way and then by rail from Fenchurch Street."

"Where is Fenchurch Street, Mr. Smith?" said I, becoming a good deal ashamed of my pertinacity.

"In the city, sir," said Mr. Smith.

The city! Now I never heard of any one in any story going out into the world to seek his fortune, and coming to a city, who did not go into it to see what was to be seen. Leaving the king's only daughter and those kinds of things, which belong to story-books, out of the question, I do not believe the captain would have passed a new city without looking into it.

"You go down the river to Fenchurch Street—in a barge?" I suggested.

"Bless ye, no, sir!" said Mr. Smith, getting the smoke of his pipe down his throat the wrong way with laughing, till I thought his coughing-fit would never allow him to give me the important information I required. "There's boats, sir, plenty on 'em. I could take you myself, and be thankful, and there's steamers calls at the wharf every quarter of an hour or so through the day, from nine in the morning, and takes you to London Bridge for threepence. It ain't many minutes' walk to Fenchurch Street, and the train takes you straight to the Docks."

After this we conversed on general seafaring matters. Mr. Smith was not a very able-bodied man, in consequence of many years' service in unhealthy climates, he said; and he complained of his trade as a "poor one," and very different from what it had been in his father's time, and before new London Bridge was built, which "anybody and anything could get through" now without watermen's assistance. In his present depressed condition he seemed to look back on his seafaring days with pride and tender regret, and when we asked for tales of his adventures he was checked by none of the scruples which withheld Mr. Rowe from encouraging me to be a sailor.

"John's berth" proved to be a truckle-bed in a closet which just held it, and which also held more nasty smells than I could have believed there was room for. Opening the window seemed only to let in fresh ones. When Fred threw himself on his face on the bed, and said, "What a beastly hole!" and cried bitterly, I was afraid he was going to be ill; and when I had said my prayers and persuaded him to say his and come to bed, I thought that if we got safely through the night we would make the return voyage with Mr. Rowe, and for the future leave events and emergencies to those who liked danger and discomfort.

But when we woke with the sun shining on our faces, and through the little window beheld it sparkling on the river below us, and on the distant city, we felt all right again, and stuck to our plans.

"Let's go by the city," said Fred, "I should like to see some of the town."

"If we don't get off before half-past nine we're lost," said I.

We found an unexpected clog in Mr. Smith, who seemed inclined to stick to us and repeat the stories he had told us overnight. At about half-past eight, however, he went off to his boat, saying he supposed we should wait for Mr. Rowe, and when his wife went into a neighbour's house I laid a shilling on the table, and Fred and I slipped out and made our way to the pier.

Mr. Rowe was not there, and a church clock near struck nine. This was echoed from the city more than once, and then we began to look anxiously for the steamer. Five, ten minutes must have passed—they seemed hours to me—when I asked a man who was waiting also when the steamer from London Bridge would come.

"She'll be here soon," said he.

"So will old Rowe," whispered Fred.

But the steamer came first, and we went on board; and the paddles began to splash, and our escape was accomplished.

It was a lovely morning, and the tall, dirty old houses looked almost grand in the sunlight as we left Nine Elms. The distant city came nearer and shone brighter, and when the fretted front of the Houses of Parliament went by us like a fairy palace, and towers and blocks of buildings rose solidly one behind another in shining tints of white and grey against the blue summer sky, and when above the noise of our paddle-wheels came the distant roar of the busy streets— Fred pressed the arm I had pushed through his and said, "We're out in the world at last!"

CHAPTER XII

EMERGENCIES AND POLICEMEN—FENCHURCH STREET STATION—THIRD CLASS TO CUSTOM HOUSE—A SHIP FOREST

Policemen are very useful people. I do not know how we should have got from the London Bridge Pier to the Fenchurch Street Station if it had not been that Fred told me he knew one could ask policemen the way to places. There is nothing to pay, which I was very glad of, as the canvas bag was getting empty.

Once or twice they helped us through emergencies. We had to go from one footpath to another, straight across the street, and the street was so full of carts and cabs and drays and omnibuses, that one could see that it was quite an impossibility. We did it, however, for the policeman made us. I said, "Hadn't we better wait till the crowd has gone?" But the policeman laughed, and said then we had better take lodgings close by and wait at the window. So we did it. Fred said the captain once ran in a little cutter between two big ships that were firing into him, but I do not think that can have been much worse than running between a backing dray, full of rolling barrels, and a hansom cab pulled up and ramping like a rocking-horse at the lowest point of the rockers.

When we were safely on the other pavement we thanked the policeman very much, and then went on, asking our way till we got to Fenchurch Street.

If anything could smell nastier than John's berth in Nine Elms it is Fenchurch Street Station. And I think it is worse in this way; John's berth smelt horrible, but it was warm and weather-tight. You never swallow a drop of pure air in Fenchurch Street Station, and yet you cannot find a corner in which you can get out of the draughts.

With one gale blowing on my right from an open door, and another gale blowing on my left down some steps, and nasty smells blowing from every point of the compass, I stood at a dirty little hole in a dirty wooden wall and took our tickets. I had to stand on tiptoe to make the young man see me.

"What is the cheapest kind of tickets you have, if you please?" I inquired, with the canvas bag in my hand.

"Third class," said the young man, staring very hard at me, which I thought rather rude. "Except working men's tickets, and they're not for this train."

"Two third-class tickets for Victoria Dock, then, if you please," said I.

"Single or return?" said he.

"I beg your pardon?" I said, for I was puzzled.

"Are you coming back to-day?" he inquired.

"Oh dear, no!" said I, for some of the captain's voyages had lasted for years; but the question made me anxious, as I knew nothing of railway rules, and I added, "Does it matter?"

"Not by no means," replied the young man smartly, and he began to whistle, but stopped himself to ask, "Custom House or Tidal Basin?"

I had no alternative but to repeat "I *beg* your pardon?"

He put his face right through the hole and looked at me. "Will you take your ticket for Custom House or Tidal Basin?" he repeated; "either will do for Victoria Docks."

"Then whichever you please," said I, as politely as I could.

The young man took out two tickets and snapped them impatiently in something; and as a fat woman was squeezing me from behind, I was glad to take what I could get and go back to Fred.

He was taking care of our two bundles and the empty pie-dish.

That pie-dish was a good deal in our way. Fred wanted to get rid of it, and said he was sure his mother would not want us to be bothered with it; but Fred had promised in his letter to bring it back, and he could not break his word. I told him so, but I said as he did not like to be seen with it I would carry it. So I did.

With a strong breeze aft, we were driven up-stairs in the teeth of a gale, and ran before a high wind down a platform where, after annoying one of the railway men very much by not being able to guess which was the train, and having to ask him, we got in among a lot of rough-looking people, who were very civil and kind. A man with a black face and a white jacket said he would tell us when we got to Custom House, and he gave me his seat by the window, that I might look out.

What struck me as rather odd was that everybody in the third-class carriage seemed to have bundles like ours, and yet they couldn't all be running away. One thin woman with a very troublesome baby had three. Perhaps it is because portmanteaus and things of that sort are rather expensive.

Fred was opposite to me. It was a bright sunny morning, a fresh breeze blew, and in the sunlight the backs of endless rows of shabby houses looked more cheerful than usual, though very few of the gardens had anything in them but dirt and cats, and very many of the windows had the week's wash hanging out on strings and poles. The villages we had passed on the canal banks all looked pretty and interesting, but I think that most of the places we saw out of the window of the train would look very ugly on a dull day.

I fancy there were poplar-trees at a place called Poplar, and that I thought it must be called after them; but Fred says No, and we have never been there since, so I cannot be sure about it. If not, I must have dreamt it.

I did fall asleep in the corner, I know, I was so very much tired, and we had had no breakfast, and I sat on the side where the wind blows in, which I think helped to make me sleepy. I was wakened partly by the pie-dish slipping off my lap, and partly by Fred saying in an eager tone,

"Oh, Charlie! LOOK! *Are they all ships*?"

We stuffed our heads through the window, and my hat was nearly blown away, so the man with the black face and the white jacket gave it to the woman with the troublesome baby to take care of for me, and he held us by our legs for fear we should fall out.

On we flew! There was wind enough in our faces to have

Juliana Horatia Ewing

filled the barge-sail three times over, and Fred licked his lips and said, "I do believe there's salt in it!"

But what he woke me up to show me drove me nearly wild. When I had seen a couple of big barges lying together with their two bare masts leaning towards each other I used to think how dignified and beautiful they looked. But here were hundreds of masts, standing as thick as tree-trunks in a fir-wood, and they were not bare poles, but lofty and slender, and crossed by innumerable yards, and covered with ropes in orderly profusion, which showed in the sunshine as cobwebs shine out in a field in summer. Gay flags and pennons fluttered in the wind; brown sails, grey sails, and gleaming white sails went up and down; and behind it all the water sparkled and dazzled our eyes like the glittering reflections from a mirror moving in the sun.

As we ran nearer the ropes looked thicker, and we could see the devices on the flags. And suddenly, straining his eyes at the yards of a vessel in the thick of the ship-forest, on which was something black, like a spider with only four legs, Fred cried, "It's a sailor!"

I saw him quite well. And seeing him higher up than on any tree one could ever climb, with the sunny sky above him and the shining water below him, I could only mutter out with envious longing—"How happy he must be!"

CHAPTER XIII

A DIRTY STREET—A BAD BOY—SHIPPING AND MERCHANDISE—WE STOWAWAY ON BOARD THE 'ATALANTA'—A SALT TEAR

The man in the white jacket helped us out, smiling as he did so, so that his teeth shone like ivory in his black face. We took the pie-dish and our bundles, and thanked him very much, and the train went on and took him with it, which we felt sorry for. For when one *is* out in the world, you know, one sometimes feels rather lonely, and sorry to part with a kind friend.

Everybody else went through a little gate into the street, so we did the same. It was a very dirty street, with houses on one side and the railway on the other. There were cabbages and carrots and old shoes and fishes' heads and oyster-shells and potato-peelings in the street, and a goat was routing among it all with its nose, as if it had lost something and hoped to find it by and by.

Places like this always seemed to depress Fred's courage. Besides which, he was never in good spirits when he had to go long without food, which made me fear he would not bear being cast adrift at sea without provisions as well as his grandfather had done. I was not surprised when he said,

Juliana Horatia Ewing

"*What* a place! And I don't believe one can get anything fit to eat, and I am so hungry!"

I looked at the houses. There was a pork-butcher's shop, and a real butcher's shop, and a slop shop, and a seedy jeweller's shop with second-hand watches, which looked as if nothing would ever make them go, and a small toy and sweetmeat shop, but not a place that looked like breakfast. I had taken Fred's bundle because he was so tired, and I suppose it was because I was staring helplessly about that a dirty boy a good deal bigger than either of us came up and pulled his dirty hair and said,

"Carry your things for you, sir?"

"No, thank you," said I, moving on with the bundles and the pie-dish; but as the boy would walk by me I said,

"We want some breakfast very much, but we haven't much money." And, remembering the cost of our supper, I added, "Could we get anything here for about twopence-half-penny or threepence apiece?"

There was a moment's pause, and then the boy gave a long whistle.

"Vy, I thought you was swells!" said he.

I really do not know whether it was because I did not like to be supposed to be a poor person when it came to the point, or whether it was because of that bad habit of mine of which even Weston's ballad has not quite cured me, of being ready to tell people more about my affairs than it can be interesting for them to hear or discreet for me to communicate, but I replied at once: "We are gentlemen; but we are going in search of adventures, and we don't want to spend more money than we can help till we see what we may want it for when we get to foreign countries."

"You're going to sea, then, *h*are you?" said the boy, keeping up with us.

"Yes," said I; "but could you tell us where to get something to eat before we go?"

"There's a shop I knows on," said our new friend, "where they sells prime pudding at a penny a slice. The plums goes all through and no mistake. Three slices would be threepence: one for you, one for him, and one for my trouble in showing you the way. Threepence more's a quart of stout, and we drink fair by turns. Shall I take your purse and pay it for you? They might cheat a stranger."

"No, thank you," said I; "but we should like some pudding if you will show us the way."

The slices were small, but then they were very heavy. We had two each. I rejected the notion of porter, and Fred said he was not thirsty; but I turned back again into the shop to ask for a glass of water for myself. The woman gave it me very civilly, looking as she did so with a puzzled manner, first at me and then at my bundles and the pie-dish. As she took back the tumbler she nodded her head towards the dirty boy, who stood in the doorway, and said,

"Is that young chap a companion of yours, my dear?"

"Oh, dear no," said I, "only he showed us the way here."

"Don't have nothing to do with him," she whispered "he's a bad un."

Juliana Horatia Ewing

In spite of this warning, however, as there was no policeman to be seen, and the boy would keep up with us, I asked him the way to Victoria Dock.

It was not so easy to get to the ships as I had expected. There were gates to pass through, and they were kept by a porter. He let some people in and turned others back.

"Have you got an order to see the docks?" asked the boy.

I confessed that we had not, but added that we wanted very much to get in.

"My eyes!" said the bad boy, doubling himself in a fit of amusement, "I believe you're both going for stowaways."

"What do you mean by stowaways?" I asked.

"Stowaways is chaps that hides aboard vessels going out of port, to get their passage free gratis for nothing."

"Do a good many manage it?" I asked with an anxious mind.

"There ain't a vessel leaves the docks without one and sometimes more aboard. The captain never looks that way, not by no accident whatsoever. He don't lift no tarpaulins while the ship's in dock. But when she gets to sea the captain gets his eyesight back, and he takes it out of the stowaways for their wittles then. Oh, yes, rather so!" said the bad boy.

There was a crowd at the gates.

"Hold your bundles down on your right side," said the boy, "and go in quickly after any respectable-looking cove you see."

Fred had got his own bundle now, and we followed our guide's directions, and went through the gates after an elderly, well-dressed man. The boy seemed to try to follow us, squeezing very close up to me, but the gatekeeper stopped him. When we were on the other side I saw him bend down and wink backwards at the gatekeeper through his straddled legs. Then he stood derisively on his head. After which he went away as a catherine-wheel, and I saw him no more.

We were among the ships at last! Vessels very different from Mr. Rowe's barge, or even the three-penny steamboat, Lofty and vast, with shining decks of marvellous cleanliness, and giant figure-heads like dismembered Jins out of some Arabian tale. Streamers of many colours high up in the forest of masts, and seamen of many nations on the decks and wharves below, moved idly in the breeze, which was redolent of many kinds of cargo. Indeed, if the choice of our ship had not been our chief care, the docks and warehouses would have fascinated us little less than the shipping. Here were huge bales of cotton packed as thickly as bricks in a brick-field. There were wine-casks innumerable, and in another place the air was aromatic with so large a cargo of coffee that it seemed as if no more could be required in this country for some generations.

It was very entertaining, and Fred was always calling to me to look at something new, but my mind was with the shipping. There was a good deal of anxiety on it too. The sooner we chose our ship and "stowed away" the better. I hesitated between sailing-vessels and steamers. I did not believe that one of the captain's adventures happened on board any ship that could move faster than it could sail. And yet I was much attracted by some grand-looking steamships. Even their huge funnels had a look of power, I thought, among the masts, like old and hollow oaks in a wood of young and slender trees.

One of these was close in dock, and we could see her well. There were some casks on deck, and by them lay a piece of tarpaulin which caught my eye, and recalled what the bad boy had said about captains and stowaways. Near the gangway were standing two men who did not seem to be sailors. They were respectably dressed, one had a book and a pencil, and they looked, I thought, as if they might have authority to ask our business in the docks, so I drew Fred back under shelter of some piled-up boxes.

"When does she sail?" asked the man with the book.

"To-morrow morning, sir," replied the other.

And then they crossed the gangway and went into a warehouse opposite.

It was noon, and being the men's dinner-time, the docks were not very busy. At this moment there was not a soul in sight. I grasped Fred's arm, and hoisted the bundle and pie-dish well under my own.

"That's our ship," I said triumphantly; "come along!"

We crossed the gangway unperceived. "The casks!" I whispered, and we made our way to the corner I had noticed. If Fred's heart beat as chokingly as mine did, we were far too much excited to speak, as we settled ourselves into a corner, not quite as cosy as our hiding-place in the forehold of the barge; and drew the tarpaulin over our heads, resting some of the weight of it on the casks behind, that we might not be smothered.

I have waited for the kitchen kettle to boil when Fred and I wanted to make "hot grog" with raspberry-vinegar and nutmeg at his father's house; I have waited for a bonfire to burn up, when we wanted to roast potatoes; I have waited for it to leave off raining when my mother would not let us go out for fear of catching colds; but I never knew time pass so slowly as when Fred and I were stowaways on board the steam-ship *Atalanta*.

He was just beginning to complain, when we heard men coming on board. This amused us for a bit, but we were stowed so that we could not see them, and we dared not look out. Neither dared we speak, except when we heard them go a good way off, and then we whispered. So second after second, and minute after minute, and hour after hour went by, and Fred became very restless.

"She's to sail in the morning," I whispered.

"But where are we to get dinner and tea and supper?" asked Fred indignantly. I was tired, and felt cross on my own account.

"You said yourself we might have to weigh out our food with a bullet like Admiral Bligh, next week."

"He must have had something, or he couldn't have weighed it," retorted Fred; "and how do we know if they'll ever give us anything to eat on board this ship?"

"I dare say we can buy food at first, till they find us something to do for our meals," said I.

"How much money is there left?" asked Fred.

I put my hand into my pocket for the canvas bag—but it was gone!

There could be little doubt that the bad boy had picked my pocket at the gate, but I had a sense of guiltiness about it, for most of the money was Fred's. This catastrophe completely overwhelmed him, and he cried and grumbled till I was nearly at my wits' end. I could not stop him, though heavy steps were coming quite close to us.

"Sh! sh!" muttered I, "if you go on like that they'll certainly find us, and then we shall have managed all this for nothing, and might as well have gone back with old Rowe."

"Which wind and weather permitting, young gentlemen, you will," said a voice just above us, though we did not hear it.

"I wish we could," sobbed Fred, "only there's no money now. But I'm going to get out of this beastly hole any way."

"You're a nice fellow to tell me about your grandfather," said I, in desperate exasperation; "I don't believe you've the pluck for a common sailor, let alone a Great Discoverer."

"You've hit the right nail on the head there, Master Charles," said the voice.

"Fiddlesticks about my grandfather!" said Fred.

In the practical experiences of the last three days my faith in Fred's tales had more than once been rather rudely shaken; but the contemptuous tone in which he disposed of our model, the Great Sea Captain, startled me so severely that I do not think I felt any additional shock of astonishment when strong hands lifted the tarpaulin from our heads, and—grave amid several grinning faces—we saw the bargemaster.

How he reproached us, and how Fred begged him to take us home, and how I besought him to let us go to sea, it would be tedious to relate. I have no doubt now that he never swerved from his intention of taking us back, but he preferred to do it by fair means if possible. So he fubbed me off, and took us round the docks to amuse us, and talked of dinner in a way that went to Fred's heart.

But when I found that we were approaching the gates once more, I stopped dead short. As we went about the docks I had replied to the barge-master's remarks as well as I could, but I had never ceased thinking of the desire of my heart, and I resolved to make one passionate appeal to his pity.

"Mr. Rowe," I said, in a choking voice, "please don't take me home! I would give anything in the world to go to sea. Why shouldn't I be a sailor when I want to? Take Fred home if he wants to go, and tell them that I'm all right, and mean to do my duty and come back a credit to them."

Mr. Rowe's face was inscrutable, and I pleaded harder.

"You're an old navy man, you know, Rowe," I said, "and if you recommended me to the captain of one of these ships for a cabin-boy, I'll be bound they'd take me."

"Mr. Charles," said the old man earnestly, "you couldn't go for a cabin-boy, you don't know—"

"You think I can't rough it," I interrupted impatiently, "but try me, and see. I know what I'm after," I added, consequentially; "and I'll bear what I have to bear, and do what I'm set to do if I can get afloat. I'll be a captain some day, and give orders instead of taking them."

Mr. Rowe drew up to attention and took off his hat. "And wanting an able-bodied seaman in them circumstances, sir, for any voyage you likes to make," said he emphatically, "call for

Samuel Rowe." He then wiped the passing enthusiasm from the crown of his head with his handkerchief, and continued—with the judicious diplomacy for which he was remarkable—"But of course, sir, it's the Royal Navy you'll begin in, as a midshipman. It's seamanship *you* wants to learn, not swabbing decks or emptying buckets below whilst others is aloft. Your father's son would be a good deal out of place, sir, as cabin-boy in a common trading vessel."

Mr. Rowe's speech made an impression, and I think he saw that it did.

"Look here, Master Charles," said he, "you've a gentleman's feelings: come home now, and bear me out with your widowed mother and your only sister, sir, and with Master Fred's father, that I'm in duty bound to, and promised to deliver safe and sound as return cargo, wind and weather permitting."

"Oh, come home! come home!" reiterated Fred.

I stood speechless for a minute or two. All around and above me rose the splendid masts, trellised with the rigging that I longed to climb. The refreshing scent of tar mingled with the smells of the various cargoes. The coming and going of men who came and went to and fro the ends of the earth stirred all my pulses to restlessness. And above the noises of their coming and going I heard the lapping of the water of the incoming tide against the dock, which spoke with a voice more powerful than that of Mr. Rowe.

And yet I went with him.

It was not because the canvas bag was empty, not because Fred would not stay with me (for I had begun to think that the captain's grandson was not destined to be the hero of exploits on the ocean), but when Mr. Rowe spoke of my widowed mother and of Henrietta, he touched a sore point on my conscience. I had had an uneasy feeling from the first that there was something rather mean in my desertion of them. Pride, and I hope some less selfish impulse, made me feel that I could never be quite happy—even on the mainmast top—if I knew that I had behaved ill to them.

I could not very well speak, but I turned round and began to walk in the direction of the dock gates. Mr. Rowe behaved uncommonly kindly. He said nothing more, but turned as if I had given the word of command, and walked respectfully just behind me. I resolved not to look back, and I did not. I was quite determined too about one thing: Mr. Rowe should never be able to say he had seen me make a fool of myself after I had made up my mind. But in reality I had very hard work to keep from beginning to cry, just when Fred was beginning to leave off.

I screwed up my eyes and kept them dry, however, but as we went through the gate there came in a sailor with a little bundle like ours, and a ship's name on his hat. His hat sat as if a gale were just taking it off, and his sea-blue shirt was blown open by breezes that my back was turned upon. In spite of all I could do one tear got through my eyelashes and ran down, and I caught it on my lips.

It was a very bitter tear, and as salt as the salt, salt sea!

CHAPTER XIV

A GLOW ON THE HORIZON—A FANTASTIC PEAL—WHAT I SAW WHEN THE ROOF FELL IN

It was the second day of our return voyage. Mr. Rowe had been very kind, and especially so to me. He had told us tales of seafaring life, but they related exclusively to the Royal Navy, and not unfrequently bore with disparagement on the mercantile marine.

Nowhere, perhaps, are grades of rank more strongly marked with professional discipline and personal independence better combined than in the army and navy. But the gulf implied by Mr. Rowe between the youngest midshipman and the highest seaman who was not an officer was, I think, in excess of the fact. As to becoming cabin-boy to a trading vessel in hopes of rising to be a captain, the barge-master contrived to impress me with the idea that I might as well take the situation of boot and knife cleaner in the Royal Kitchen, in hopes of its proving the first step towards ascending the Throne.

We seemed to have seen and done so much since we were on the canal before, that I felt quite sentimental as we glided into Linnet Flash.

"The old place looks just the same, Barge-master," said I with a travelled air.

"So it do, sir," said Mr. Rowe; and he added—"There's no place like Home."

I hardly know how near we were to the town, but I know that it was getting late, that the dew was heavy on the towing-path, and that among the dark pencilled shadows of the sallows in the water the full moon's reflection lay like a golden shield; when the driver, who was ahead, stepped back and shouted—"The bells are ringing!"

When we got a little nearer we heard them quite clearly, and just when I was observing a red glow diffuse itself in the cold night sky above the willow hedge on our left, Mr. Rowe said, "There must be a queer kind of echo somewhere, I heard sixteen bells."

And then I saw the driver, whose figure stood out dark against the moonlit moorland on our right, point with his arm to the fast crimsoning sky, and Mr. Rowe left the rudder and came forward, and Fred, who had had his head low down listening, ran towards us from the bows and cried,

"There *are* sixteen, and they're ringing backwards—*it's a fire!*"

The driver mounted the horse, which was put to the trot, and we hurried on. The bells came nearer and nearer with their fantastic clanging, and the sky grew more lurid as they rang. Then there was a bend in the canal, and we caught sight of the two towers of S. Philip and S. James, dark against the glow.

"The whole town is in flames!" cried Fred.

"Not it," said the barge-master; "it's ten to one nothing but a rubbish-heap burning, or the moors on fire beyond the town."

Mr. Rowe rather snubbed Fred, but I think he was curious about the matter. The driver urged his horse, and the good barge *Betsy* swung along at a pace to which she was little accustomed.

When we came by the cricket-field Mr. Rowe himself said— "It's in the middle of the town."

Through the deafening noise of the bells I contrived to shout in his ear a request that I might be put ashore, as we were now about on a level with my home. Mr. Rowe ran a plank quickly out and landed me, without time for adieux.

I hastened up to the town. The first street I got into was empty, but it seemed to vibrate to S. Philip's peal. And after that I pushed my way through people, hurrying as I was hurrying, and the nearer I got to home the thicker grew the crowd and the ruddier became the glow. And now, in spite of the bells, I caught other noises. The roar of irresistible fire,— which has a strange likeness to the roar of irresistible water,—the loud crackling of the burning wood, and the moving and talking of the crowd, which was so dense that I could hardly get forward.

I contrived to squeeze myself along, however, and as I turned into our street I felt the warmth of the fire, and when I looked at my old home it was a mass of flames.

I tried to get people to make way for me by saying—"It's my house, please let me through!" But nobody seemed to hear me. And yet there was a pause, which was only filled by that curious sound when a crowd of people gasp or sigh; and if every man had been a rock it could not have been more impossible to move backwards or forwards. It was dark, except for the moonlight, where I stood, but in a moment or two the flames burst from the bedroom windows, and the red light spread farther, and began to light up faces near me. I was just about to appeal to a man I knew, when a roar began which I knew was not that of the fire. It was the roar of human voices. And when it swelled louder, and was caught up as it came along, and then broke into deafening cheers, I was so wild with excitement and anxiety that I began to kick the legs of the man in front of me to make him let me go to the home that was burning before my eyes.

What he would have done in return, I don't know, but at this moment the crowd broke up, and we were pushed, and pressed, and jostled about, and people kept calling to "Make way!" and after tumbling down, and being picked up twice, I found myself in the front row of a kind of lane that had been made through the crowd, down which several men were coming, carrying on their shoulders an arm-chair with people in it.

As they passed me there was a crash, which seemed to shake the street. The roof of our house had fallen in!

As it fell the flames burst upon every side, and in the sudden glare the street became as bright as day, and every little thing about one seemed to spring into sight. Half the crowd was known to me in a moment.

Then I looked at the chair which was being carried along; and by a large chip on one of the legs I knew it was my father's old arm-chair.

And in the chair I saw Rupert in his shirt and trousers, and Henrietta in a petticoat and an out-door jacket, with so white a face that even the firelight seemed to give it no colour, and on her lap was Baby Cecil in his night-gown, with black smut marks on his nose and chin.

CHAPTER XV

HENRIETTA'S DIARY—A GREAT EMERGENCY

Rupert never was a fellow who could give descriptions of things, and Henrietta was ill for some time after the fire, and Mr. Bustard said she wasn't to talk about it.

But she knew I wanted to know, so one day when she was down-stairs with me in the "Miniature Room" (it was at the Castle) she gave me a manuscript book, and said, "It's my diary, Charlie, so I know you won't look. But I've put in two marks for the beginning and end of the bit about the fire. I wrote it that evening, you know, before Mr. Bustard came, and my head got so bad."

Of course I made her show me exactly where to begin and leave off, and then I read it. This was it.

"It had been a very hot day, and I had got rather a headache and gone to bed. The pain kept me awake a good bit, and when I did get to sleep I think I slept rather lightly. I was partly awakened by noises which seemed to have been going in my head all night till I could bear them no longer, so I woke up, and found that people were shouting outside, and that there was a dreadful smell of burning. I had got on my flannel petticoat when Rupert called me and said, 'Henny dear, the house is on fire! Just put something round you, and come quickly.'"

"Just outside the door we met Cook; she said, 'The Lord be thanked! it's you, Miss Henrietta. Come along!'"

"Rupert said, 'Where's Mother, Cook?'"

"'Missus was took with dreadful fainting fits,' she replied, 'and they've got her over to the *Crown*. We're all to go there, and everything that can be saved.'"

"'Where's Baby,' said I, 'and Jane?'"

"'With your Ma, miss, I expect,' Cook said; and as we came out she asked some one, who said, 'I saw Jane at the door of the *Crown* just now.' I had been half asleep till then, but when we got into the street and saw the smoke coming out of the dining-room window, Rupert and I wanted to stay and try to save something, but one of the men who was there said, 'You and your brother's not strong enough to be of no great use, miss; you're only in the way of the engine. Everybody's doing their best to save your things, and if you'll go to the *Crown* to your mamma, you'll do the best that could be.'"

"The people who were saving our things saved them all alike. They threw them out of the window, and as I had seen the big blue china jar smashed to shivers, I felt a longing to go and show them what to do; but Rupert said, 'The fellow's quite right, Henny,' and he seized me by the hand and dragged me off to the *Crown*. Jane was in the hall, looking quite wild, and she said to us, 'Where's Master Cecil?' I didn't stop to ask her how it was that she didn't know. I ran out again, and Rupert came after me. I suppose we both looked up at the nursery window when we came near, and there was Baby Cecil standing and screaming for help. Before we got to the door other people had seen him, and two or three men pushed into the house. They came out gasping and puffing without Cecil, and I heard one man say, 'It's too far gone. It wouldn't bear a child's weight, and if you got up you'd never come down again.'"

"'God help the poor child!' said the other man, who was the chemist, and had a large family, I know. I looked round and saw by Rupert's face that he had heard. It was like a stone. I don't know how it was, but it seemed to come into my head: 'If Baby Cecil is burnt it will kill Rupert too.' And I began to think; and I thought of the back stairs. There was a pocket-handkerchief in my jacket pocket, and I soaked it in the water on the ground. The town burgesses wouldn't buy a new hose when we got the new steam fire-engine, and when they used the old one it burst in five places, so that everything was swimming, for the water was laid on from the canal. I think my idea must have been written on my face, for though I didn't speak, Rupert seemed to guess at once, and he ran after me, crying, 'Let me go, Henrietta!' but I pretended not to hear.

"When we got to the back of the house the fire was not nearly so bad, and we got in. But though it wasn't exactly on fire where we were, the smoke came rolling down the passage from the front of the house, and by the time we got to the back stairs we could not see or breathe, in spite of wet cloths over our faces, and our eyes smarted with the smoke. Go down on all fours, Henny,' said Rupert. So I did. It was wonderful. When I got down with my face close to the ground there was a bit of quite fresh air, and above this the smoke rolled like a cloud. I could see the castors of the legs of a table in the hall, but no higher up. In this way we saw the foot of the back stairs, and climbed up them on our hands and knees. But in spite of the bit of fresh air near the ground the smoke certainly grew thicker, and it got hotter and hotter, and we could hear the roaring of the flames coming nearer, and the clanging of the bells outside, and I never knew what it was to feel thirst before then! When we were up the first flight, and the smoke was suffocating, I heard Rupert say, 'Oh, Henny, you good girl, shall we ever get down again!' I couldn't speak, my throat was so sore, but I remember thinking, 'It's like going up through the clouds into heaven; and we shall find Baby Cecil there.' But after that it got rather clearer, because the fire was in the lower part of the house then, and when we got to the top we stood up, and found our way to the nursery by hearing Baby Cecil scream.

"The great difficulty was to get him down, for we couldn't carry him and keep close to the ground. So I said, 'You go first on your hands and knees backwards, and tell him to do as you do, and I'll come last, so that he may see me doing the same and imitate me.' Baby was very good about it, and when the heat worried him and he stopped, Rupert said, 'Come on, Baby, or Henny will run over you,' and he scrambled down as good as gold.

"And when we got to the door the people began to shout and to cheer, and I thought they would have torn Baby to bits. It made me very giddy, and so did the clanging of those dreadful bells; and then I noticed that Rupert was limping, and I said, 'Oh, Rupert, have you hurt your knee?' and he said, 'It's nothing, come to the *Crown*.' But there were two of the young men from Jones's shop there, and they said, 'Don't you walk and hurt your knee, sir; we'll take you.' And they pushed up my father's arm-chair, which had been saved and was outside, and Rupert sat down, I believe, because he could not stand. Then they said, 'There's room for you, miss,' and Rupert told me to come, and I took Baby on my lap; but I felt so ill I thought I should certainly fall out when they lifted us up.

"The way the people cheered made me very giddy; I think I shall always feel sick when I hear hurrahing now."

"Rupert is very good if you're ill. He looked at me and said, 'You're the bravest girl I ever knew, but don't faint if you can help it, or Baby will fall out.'"

"I didn't; and I wouldn't have fainted when we got to the *Crown if I could have stopped myself by anything I could do.*"

CHAPTER XVI

MR. ROWE ON THE SUBJECT—OUR COUSIN— WESTON GETS INTO PRINT—THE HARBOUR'S MOUTH—WHAT LIES BEYOND

Mr. Rowe's anxiety to see Rupert and Henrietta, and to "take the liberty of expressing himself" about their having saved Baby Cecil's life was very great, but the interview did not take place for some time. The barge *Betsy* took two voyages to Nine Elms and home again before Henrietta was downstairs and allowed to talk about the fire.

Rupert refused to see the barge-master when he called to ask after Henrietta; he was vexed because people made a fuss about the affair, and when Rupert was vexed he was not gracious. When Henrietta got better, however, she said, "We ought to see old Rowe and thank him for his kindness to Charlie;" so the next time he called, we all went into the housekeeper's room to see him.

He was very much pleased and excited, which always seemed to make him inclined to preach. He set forth the noble motives which must have moved Rupert and Henrietta to their heroic conduct in the emergency, so that I felt more proud of them than ever. But Rupert frowned, and said, "Nonsense, Rowe, I'm sure I never thought anything of the kind. I don't believe we either of us thought anything at all."

But Mr. Rowe had not served seventeen years in the Royal Navy to be put down when he expounded a point of valour.

"That's where it is, Master Rupert," said he. "It wouldn't have been you or Miss Henrietta either if you had. 'A man overboard,' says you—that's enough for one of your family, sir. *They* never stops to think 'Can I swim?' but in you goes, up the stairs that wouldn't hold the weight of a new-born babby, and right through the raging flames."

"Oh, dear!" cried Henrietta, "that's just what Cook and all kinds of people will say. But it was the front stairs that were on fire. We only went up the back stairs, and they weren't burning at all."

The barge-master smiled in reply. But it was with the affability of superior knowledge, and I feel quite sure that he always told the story (and believed it) according to his impossible version.

It was on the third day after the fire that our cousin called at the *Crown*. He had never been to see us before, and, as I have said, we had never been to the Castle. But the next day he sent a close carriage for Henrietta and my mother, and a dog-cart for Rupert and me, and brought us up to the Castle. We were there for three months.

It was through him that Rupert went to those baths abroad, which cured his knee completely. And then, because my mother could not afford to do it, he sent him to a grander public school than Dr. Jessop's old grammar school, and Mr. Johnson sent Thomas Johnson there too, for Tom could not bear to be parted from Rupert, and his father never refused him anything.

Juliana Horatia Ewing

But what I think was so very kind of our cousin was his helping me. Rupert and Henrietta had been a credit to the family, but I deserved nothing. I had only run away in the mean hope of outshining them, and had made a fool of myself, whilst they had been really great in doing their duty at home. However, he did back me up with Mother about going to sea, and got me on board the training-ship *Albion*; and my highest hope is to have the chance of bringing my share of renown to my father's name, that his cousin may never regret having helped me to my heart's desire.

Fred Johnson and I are very good friends, but since our barge voyage we have never been quite so intimate. I think the strongest tie between us was his splendid stories of the captain, and I do not believe in them now.

Oddly enough, my chief friend—of the whole lot—is Weston. Rupert always said I had a vulgar taste in the choice of friends, so it seems curious that of our old schoolmates Johnson should be his friend and Weston mine. For Johnson's father is only a canal-carrier, and Weston is a fellow of good family.

He is so very clever! And I have such a habit of turning my pockets inside out for everybody to see, that I admire his reticence; and then, though he is so ironical with himself, as well as other people, he has very fine ideas and ambitions and very noble and upright principles—when you know him well.

"It's an ill wind that blows nobody good," and the fire that burned down our house got Weston into print at last.

It was not a common letter either, in the "correspondence" part, with small type, and the editor not responsible. It was a leading article, printed big, and it was about the fire and

Rupert and Henrietta. Thomas Johnson read it to us, and we did not know who wrote it; but it was true, and in good taste. After the account of the fire came a quotation from Horace,

"Fortes creantur fortibus et bonis."

And Johnson cried—"That's Weston, depend upon it. He's in the *Weekly Spectator* at last!"

And then, to my utter amazement, came such a chronicle of the valiant deeds of Rupert's ancestors as Weston could only have got from one source. What had furnished his ready pen with matter for a comic ballad to punish my bragging had filled it also to do honour to Rupert and Henrietta's real bravery, and down to what the colonel of my father's regiment had said of him—it was all there.

Weston came to see me the other day at Dartmouth, where our training-ship *Albion* lies, and he was so charmed by the old town with its carved and gabled houses, and its luxuriant gardens rich with pale-blossomed laurels, which no frost dwarfs, and crimson fuchsias gnarled with age, and its hill-embosomed harbour, where the people of all grades and ages, and of both sexes, flit hither and thither in their boats as landlubbers would take an evening stroll—that I felt somewhat justified in the romantic love I have for the place.

And when we lay in one of the *Albion's* boats, rocking up and down in that soothing swell which freshens the harbour's mouth, Weston made me tell him all about the lion and the silver chain, and he called me a prig for saying so often that I did not believe in it now. I remember he said, "In this sleepy, damp, delightful Dartmouth, who but a prig could deny the truth of a poetical dream?"

He declared he could see the lion in a cave in the rock, and

Juliana Horatia Ewing

that the poor beast wanted a new sea-green ribbon.

Weston speaks so much more cleverly than I can, that I could not explain to him then that I am still but too apt to dream! But the harbour's mouth is now only the beginning of my visions, which stretch far over the sea beyond, and over the darker line of that horizon where the ships come and go.

I hope it is not wrong to dream. My father was so modest as well as ambitious, so good as well as so gallant, that I would rather die than disgrace him by empty conceit and unprofitable hopes.

Weston is a very religious fellow, though he does not "cant" at all. When I was going away to Dartmouth, and he saw me off (for we were great friends), one of the last things he said to me was, "I say, don't leave off saying your prayers, you know."

I haven't, and I told him so this last time. I often pray that if ever I am great I may be good too; and sometimes I pray that if I try hard to be good God will let me be great as well.

The most wonderful thing was old Rowe's taking a cheap ticket and coming down to see me last summer. I never can regret my voyage with him in the *Betsy*, for I did thoroughly enjoy it, though I often think how odd it is that in my vain, jealous wild-goose chase after adventures I missed the chance of distinguishing myself in the only Great Emergency which has yet occurred in our family.

A VERY ILL-TEMPERED FAMILY

"Finding, following, keeping, struggling,
Is HE sure to bless?"

—Hymn of the Eastern Church

CHAPTER I

A FAMILY FAILING

We are a very ill-tempered family.

I want to say it, and not to unsay it by any explanations, because I think it is good for us to face the fact in the unadorned form in which it probably presents itself to the minds of our friends.

Amongst ourselves we have always admitted it by pieces, as it were, or in negative propositions. We allow that we are firm of disposition; we know that we are straightforward; we show what we feel. We have opinions and principles of our own; we are not so thick-skinned as some good people, nor as cold-blooded as others.

When two of us quarrelled (and Nurse used to say that no two of us ever agreed), the provocation always seemed, to each of us, great enough amply to excuse the passion. But I have reason to think that people seldom exclaimed, "What grievances those poor children are exasperated with!" but that they often said, "What terrible tempers they all have!"

There are five of us: Philip and I are the eldest; we are twins. My name is Isobel, and I never allow it to be shortened into the ugly word *Bella* nor into the still more hideous word *Izzy*, by either the servants or the children. My aunt Isobel never would, and neither will I.

"The children" are the other three. They are a good deal younger than Philip and I, so we have always kept them in order. I do not mean that we taught them to behave wonderfully well, but I mean that we made them give way to us elder ones. Among themselves they squabbled dreadfully.

We are a very ill-tempered family.

CHAPTER II

ILL-TEMPERED PEOPLE AND THEIR FRIENDS—
NARROW ESCAPES—THE HATCHET-QUARREL

I do not wish for a moment to defend ill-temper, but I do think that people who suffer from ill-tempered people often talk as if they were the only ones who do suffer in the matter; and as if the ill-tempered people themselves quite enjoyed being in a rage.

And yet how much misery is endured by those who have never got the victory over their own ill-temper! To feel wretched and exasperated by little annoyances which good-humoured people get over with a shrug or a smile; to have things rankle in my mind like a splinter in the flesh, which glide lightly off yours, and leave no mark; to be unable to bear a joke, knowing that one is doubly laughed at because one can't; to have this deadly sore at heart—"I *cannot* forgive; I *cannot* forget," there is no pleasure in these things. The tears of sorrow are not more bitter than the tears of anger, of hurt pride or thwarted will. As to the fit of passion in which one is giddy, blind, and deaf, if there is a relief to the overcharged mind in saying the sharpest things and hitting the heaviest blows one can at the moment, the pleasantness is less than momentary, for almost as we strike we foresee the pains of regret and of humbling ourselves to beg pardon which must ensue. Our friends do not always pity as well as blame us, though they are sorry for those who were possessed by devils long ago.

Good-tempered people, too, who I fancy would find it quite easy not to be provoking, and to be a little patient and forbearing, really seem sometimes to irritate hot-tempered ones on purpose, as if they thought it was good for them to get used to it.

I do not mean that I think ill-tempered people should be constantly yielded to, as Nurse says Mrs. Rampant and the servants have given way to Mr. Rampant till he has got to be quite as unreasonable and nearly as dangerous as most maniacs, and his friends never cross him, for the same reason that they would hot stir up a mad bull.

Perhaps I do not quite know how I would have our friends treat us who are cursed with bad tempers. I think to avoid unnecessary provocation, and to be patient with us in the height of our passion, is wise as well as kind. But no principle should be conceded to us, and rights that we have unjustly attacked should be faithfully defended when we are calm enough to listen. I fancy that where gentle Mrs. Rampant is wrong is that she allows Mr. Rampant to think that what really are concessions to his weakness are concessions to his wisdom. And what is not founded on truth cannot do lasting good. And if, years ago, before he became a sort of gunpowder cask at large, he had been asked if he wished Mrs. Rampant to persuade herself, and Mrs. Rampant, the little Rampants, and the servants to combine to persuade him, that he was right when he was wrong, and wise when he was foolish, and reasonable when he was unjust, I think he would have said No. I do not believe one could deliberately desire to be befooled by one's family for all the best years of one's life. And yet how many people are!

I do not think I am ever likely to be so loved and feared by those I live with as to have my ill-humours made into laws. I hope not. But I am sometimes thankful, on the other hand, that GOD is more forbearing with us than we commonly are with each other, and does not lead us into temptation when we are at our worst and weakest.

Any one who has a bad temper must sometimes look back at the years before he learned self-control, and feel thankful that he is not a murderer, or burdened for life by the weight on his conscience of some calamity of which he was the cause. If the knife which furious Fred threw at his sister before he was out of petticoats had hit the child's eye instead of her forehead, could he ever have looked into the blinded face without a pang? If the blow with which impatient Annie flattered herself she was correcting her younger brother had thrown the naughty little lad out of the boat instead of into the sailor's arms, and he had been drowned—at ten years old a murderess, how could she endure for life the weight of her unavailing remorse?

I very nearly killed Philip once. It makes me shudder to think of it, and I often wonder I ever could lose my temper again.

We were eight years old, and out in the garden together. We had settled to build a moss-house for my dolls, and had borrowed the hatchet out of the wood-house, without leave, to chop the stakes with. It was entirely my idea, and I had collected all the moss and most of the sticks. It was I, too, who had taken the hatchet. Philip had been very tiresome about not helping me in the hard part; but when I had driven in the sticks by leaning on them with all my weight, and had put in bits of brushwood where the moss fell out and Philip laughed at me, and, in short, when the moss-house was beginning to look quite real, Philip was very anxious to work at it, and wanted the hatchet.

"You wouldn't help me over the hard work," said I, "so I shan't give it you now; I'll make my moss-house myself."

"No, you won't," said Philip.

"Yes, I shall," said I.

"No, you won't," he reiterated; "for I shall pull it down as fast as you build it."

"You'd better not," I threatened.

Just then we were called in to dinner. I hid the hatchet, and Philip said no more; but he got out before me, and when I returned to work I found that the moss-house walls, which had cost me so much labour, were pulled to pieces and scattered about the shrubbery. Philip was not to be seen.

My heart had been so set upon my project that at first I could only feel the overwhelming disappointment. I was not a child who often cried, but I burst into tears.

I was sobbing my hardest when Philip sprang upon me in triumph, and laughing at my distress.

"I kept my promise," said he, tossing his head, "and I'll go on doing it."

I am sure those shocks of fury which seize one like a fit must be a devil possessing one. In an instant my eyes were as dry as the desert in a hot wind, and my head reeling with passion. I ran to the hatchet, and came back brandishing it.

"If you touch one stake or bit of moss of mine again," said I, "I'll throw my hatchet at your head. I can keep promises too."

My intention was only to frighten him. I relied on his not daring to brave such a threat; unhappily he relied on my not daring to carry it out. He took up some of my moss and threw it at me by way of reply.

I flung the hatchet!—

My Aunt Isobel has a splendid figure, with such grace and power as one might expect from her strong health and ready mind. I had not seen her at the moment, for I was blind with passion, nor had Philip, for his back was turned towards her. I did not see distinctly how she watched, as one watches for a ball, and caught the hatchet within a yard of Philip's head.

My Aunt Isobel has a temper much like the temper of the rest of the family. When she had caught it in her left hand she turned round and boxed my ears with her right hand till I could see less than ever. (I believe she suffered for that outburst for months afterwards. She was afraid she had damaged my hearing, as that sense is too often damaged or destroyed by the blows of ill-tempered parents, teachers, and nurses.)

Then she turned back and shook Philip as vigorously as she had boxed me. "I saw you, you spiteful, malicious boy!" said my Aunt Isobel.

All the time she was shaking him, Philip was looking at her feet. Something that he saw absorbed his attention so fully that he forgot to cry.

"You're bleeding, Aunt Isobel," said he, when she gave him breath enough to speak.

The truth was this: the nervous force which Aunt Isobel had summoned up to catch the hatchet seemed to cease when it was caught; her arm fell powerless, and the hatchet cut her ankle. That left arm was useless for many months afterwards, to my abiding reproach.

Philip was not hurt, but he might have been killed. Everybody told me so often that it was a warning to me to correct my terrible temper, that I might have revolted against the reiteration if the facts had been less grave. But I never can feel lightly about that hatchet-quarrel. It opened a gulf of possible wickedness and life-long misery, over the brink of which my temper would have dragged me, but for Aunt Isobel's strong arm and keen eye, and over which it might succeed in dragging me any day, unless I could cure myself of my besetting sin.

I never denied it. It was a warning.

CHAPTER III

WARNINGS—MY AUNT ISOBEL—
MR. RAMPANT'S TEMPER, AND HIS CONSCIENCE

I was not the only scarecrow held up before my own mind.

Nurse had a gallery of historical characters, whom she kept as beacons to warn our stormy passions of their fate. The hot-tempered boy who killed his brother when they were at school; the hot-tempered farmer who took his gun to frighten a trespasser, and ended by shooting him; the young lady who destroyed the priceless porcelain in a pet; the hasty young gentleman who kicked his favourite dog and broke its ribs;— they were all warnings: so was old Mr. Rampant, so was my Aunt Isobel.

Aunt Isobel's story was a whispered tradition of the nursery for many years before she and I were so intimate, in consequence of her goodness and kindness to me, that one day I was bold enough to say to her, "Aunt Isobel, is it true that the reason why you never married is because you and he quarrelled, and you were very angry, and he went away, and he was drowned at sea?"

Child as I was, I do not think I should have been so indelicate as to have asked this question if I had not come to

Juliana Horatia Ewing

fancy that Nurse made out the story worse than it really was, for my behoof. Aunt Isobel was so cheerful and bright with us!—and I was not at that time able to believe that any one could mend a broken heart with other people's interests so that the marks should show so little!

My aunt had a very clear skin, but in an instant her face was thick with a heavy blush, and she was silent. I marvelled that these were the only signs of displeasure she allowed herself to betray, for the question was no sooner out of my mouth than I wished it unsaid, and felt how furious she must naturally feel to hear that her sad and sacred story was bandied between servants and children as a nursery-tale with a moral to it.

But oh, Aunt Isobel! Aunt Isobel! you had at this time progressed far along that hard but glorious road of self-conquest which I had hardly found my way to.

"I beg your pardon," I began, before she spoke.

"You ought to," said my aunt—she never spoke less than decisively—"I thought you had more tact, Isobel, than to tell any one what servants have said of one's sins or sorrows behind one's back."

"I am *very* sorry," I repeated with shame; "but the thing is, I didn't believe it was true, you always seem so happy. I am *very* sorry."

"It is true," said Aunt Isobel. "Child, whilst we are speaking of it—for the first and the last time—let it be a warning for you to illustrate a very homely proverb: 'Don't cut off your nose to spite your own face.' Ill-tempered people are always doing it, and I did it to my life-long loss. I *was* angry with him, and like Jonah I said to myself, 'I do well to be angry.'

And though I would die twenty deaths harder than the death he died to see his face for five minutes and be forgiven, I am not weak enough to warp my judgment with my misery. I was in the right, and he was in the wrong. But I forgot how much harder a position it is to be in the wrong than in the right in a quarrel. I did not think of how, instead of making the return path difficult to those who err, we ought to make it easy, as GOD does for us. I gave him no chance of unsaying with grace or credit what he could not fail to regret that he had said. Isobel, you have a clear head and a sharp tongue, as I have. You will understand when I say that I had the satisfaction of proving that I was in the right and he was in the wrong, and that I was firmly, conscientiously determined to make no concessions, no half-way advances, though our Father *goes to meet* His prodigals. Merciful Heaven! I had the satisfaction of parting myself for all these slow years from the most honest—the tenderest-hearted—"

My Aunt Isobel had overrated her strength. After a short and vain struggle in silence she got up and went slowly out of the room, resting her hand for an instant on my little knick-knack table by the door as she went out—the only time I ever saw her lean upon anything.

* * * * *

Old Mr. Rampant was another of my "warnings." He—to whose face no one dared hint that he could ever be in the wrong—would have been more astonished than Aunt Isobel to learn how plainly—nay, how contemptuously—the servants spoke behind his back of his unbridled temper and its results. They knew that the only son was somewhere on the other side of the world, and that little Mrs. Rampant wept tears for him and sent money to him in secret, and they had no difficulty in deciding why: "He'd got his father's temper, and it stood to reason that he and the old gentleman couldn't

Juliana Horatia Ewing

put up their horses together." The moral was not obscure. From no lack of affection, but for want of self-control, the son was condemned to homelessness and hardships in his youth, and the father was sonless in his old age.

But that was not the point of Nurse's tales about Mr. Rampant which impressed me most, nor even the endless anecdotes of his unreasonable passions which leaked out at his back-door and came up our back-stairs to the nursery. They rather amused us. That assault on the butcher's boy, who brought ribs of beef instead of sirloin, for which he was summoned and fined; his throwing the dinner out of the window, and going to dine at the village inn—by which the dogs ate the dinner and he had to pay for two dinners, and to buy new plates and dishes.

We laughed at these things, but in my serious moments, especially on the first Sunday of the month, I was haunted by something else which Nurse had told me about old Mr. Rampant.

In our small parish—a dull village on the edge of a marsh—the Holy Communion was only celebrated once a month. It was not because he was irreligious that old Mr. Rampant was one of the too numerous non-communicants. "It's his temper, poor gentleman," said Nurse. "He can't answer for himself, and he has that religious feeling he wouldn't like to come unless he was fit. The housekeeper overheard Mrs. Rampant a-begging of him last Christmas. It was no listening either, for he bellowed at her like a bull, and swore dreadful that whatever else he was he wouldn't be profane."

"Couldn't he keep his temper for a week, don't you think?" said I sadly, thinking of my mother's old copy of the *Weeks Preparation* for the Lord's Supper.

"It would be as bad if he got into one of his tantrums directly afterwards," said Nurse: "and with people pestering for Christmas-boxes, and the pudding and turkey, and so many things that might go wrong, it would be as likely as not he would. It's a sad thing too," she added, "for his neck's terribly short, and they say all his family have gone suddenly with the apoplexy. It's an awful thing, Miss Isobel, to be taken sudden—and unprepared."

The awe of it came back on me every month when the fair white linen covered the rustiness of the old velvet altar-cloth which the marsh damps were rotting, and the silver vessels shone, and the village organist played out the non-communicants with a somewhat inappropriate triumphal march, and little Mrs. Rampant knelt on with buried face as we went out, and Mr. Rampant came out with us, looking more glum than usual, and with such a short neck!

Now I think poor Mr. Rampant was wrong, and that he ought to have gone with Mrs. Rampant to the Lord's Supper that Christmas. He might have found grace to have got through all the little ups and downs and domestic disturbances of a holiday season without being very ferocious; and if he had tried and failed I think GOD would have forgiven him. And he might—it is possible that he *might*—during that calm and solemn Communion, have forgiven his son as he felt that Our Father forgave him. So Aunt Isobel says; and I have good reason to think that she is likely to be right.

I think so too *now*, but *then* I was simply impressed by the thought that an ill-tempered person was, as Nurse expressed it, "unfit" to join in the highest religious worship. It is true that I was also impressed by her other saying, "It's an awful thing, Miss Isobel, to be taken sudden and unprepared;" but there was a temporary compromise in my own case. I could not be a communicant till I was confirmed.

CHAPTER IV

CASES OF CONSCIENCE— ETHICS OF ILL-TEMPER

Confirmations were not very frequent in our little village at this time. About once in three years the Bishop came to us. He came when I was twelve years old. Opinions were divided as to whether I was old enough, but I decided the matter by saying I would rather wait till the next opportunity.

"I may be more fit by that time," was my thought, and it was probably not unlike some of Mr. Rampant's self-communings.

The time came, and the Bishop also; I was fifteen.

I do not know why, but nobody had proposed that Philip should be confirmed at twelve years old. Fifteen was thought to be quite early enough for him, and so it came about that we were confirmed together.

I am very thankful that, as it happened, I had Aunt Isobel to talk to.

"You're relieved from one perplexity at any rate," said she, when I had been speaking of that family failing which was also mine. "You know your weak point. I remember a long talk I had, years ago, with Mrs. Rampant, whom I used to know very well when we were young. She said one of her great difficulties was not being able to find out her besetting sin. She said it always made her so miserable when clergymen preached on that subject, and said that every enlightened Christian must have discovered one master passion amongst the others of his soul. She had tried so hard, and could only find a lot, none much bigger or much less than the others. Some vanity, some selfishness, some distrust and weariness, some peevishness, some indolence, and a lapful of omissions. Since she married," continued my aunt, slowly pulling her thick black eyelashes, after a fashion she had, "I believe she has found the long-lost failing. It is impatience with Mr. Rampant, she thinks."

I could not help laughing.

"However, Isobel, we may be sure of this, people of soft, gentle temperaments have their own difficulties with their own souls which we escape. Perhaps in the absence of such marked vices as bring one to open shame one might be slower to undertake vigorous self-improvement. You and I have no difficulty in seeing the sin lying at *our* door."

"N—no," said I.

"Well, *have you*?" said Aunt Isobel, facing round. "Bless me," she added impetuously, "don't say you haven't if you have. Never let any one else think for you, child!"

"If you'll only have patience and let me explain—"

"I'm patience its very self!" interrupted my aunt, "but I do hate a No that means Yes."

My patience began to evaporate.

"There are some things, Aunt Isobel, *you know*, which can't be exactly squeezed into No and Yes. But if you don't want to be bothered I won't say anything, or I'll say yes or no, which ever you like."

And I kicked the shovel. (My aunt had shoved the poker with *her* slipper.) She drew her foot back and spoke very gently:

"I beg your pardon, my dear. Please say what you were going to say, and in your own way."

There is no doubt that good-humour—like bad—is infectious. I drew nearer to Aunt Isobel, and fingered the sleeve of her dress caressingly.

"You know, dear Aunt Isobel, that I should never think of saying to the Rector what I want to say to you. And I don't mean that I don't agree to whatever he tells us about right and wrong, but still I think if one can be quite convinced in the depths of one's own head, too, it's a good thing, as well as knowing that he must be right."

"Certainly," said Aunt Isobel.

"To begin with, I don't want you to think me any better than I am. When we were very very little, Philip and I used to spit at each other, and pull each other's hair out. I do not do nasty or unladylike things now when I am angry, but, Aunt Isobel, my 'besetting sin' is not conquered, it's only civilized."

"I quite agree with you," said Aunt Isobel; which rather annoyed me. I gulped this down, however, and went on:

"The sin of ill-temper, *if it is a sin*," I began. I paused, expecting an outburst, but Aunt Isobel sat quite composedly, and fingered her eyelashes.

"Of course the Rector would be horrified if I said such a thing at the confirmation-class," I continued, in a dissatisfied tone.

"Don't invent grievances, Isobel, for I see you have a real stumbling-block, when we can come to it. You are not at the confirmation-class, and I am not easily horrified."

"Well, there are two difficulties—I explain very stupidly," said I with some sadness.

"We'll take them one at a time," replied Aunt Isobel with an exasperating blandness, which fortunately stimulated me to plain-speaking.

"Everybody says one ought to 'restrain' one's temper, but I'm not sure if I think one ought. Isn't it better to *have things out*? Look at Philip. He's going to be confirmed, and then he'll go back to school, and when he and another boy quarrel, they'll fight it out, and feel comfortable afterwards. Aunt Isobel, I can quite understand feeling friendly after you've had it out, even if you're the one who is beaten, if it has been a fair fight. Now *restraining* your temper means forcing yourself to be good outside, and feeling all the worse inside, and feeling it longer. There is that utterly stupid little school-room-maid, who is under my orders, that I may teach her. Aunt Isobel, you would not credit how often I tell her the same thing, and how politely she says 'Yes, miss!' and how invariably she doesn't do it after all. I say, 'You *know* I told you only yesterday. What *is* the use of my trying to teach you?' and all kinds of mild things like that; but really I quite hate her for giving me so much trouble and taking so little herself, and I wish I might discharge her. Now, if only it wasn't wrong to throw—what are those things hot-tempered gentlemen always throw at their servants?"

"Don't ask me, my dear; ask Mr. Rampant."

"Oh, he throws everything. Bootjacks—that's it. Now, if only I might throw a bootjack at her, it would waken her up, and be such a relief to my feelings, that I shouldn't feel half so unforgiving towards her all along. Then as to swearing, Aunt Isobel—"

"Swearing!" ejaculated my aunt.

"Of course swearing is very wrong, and all profane-speaking but I do think it *would be* a help if there was some innocent kind of strong language to use when one feels strongly."

"If we didn't use up all our innocent strong language by calling things awful and horrible that have not an element of awe or horror in them, we should have some left for our great occasions," said Aunt Isobel.

"Perhaps," said I, "but that's not exactly what I mean. Now do you think it would be wrong to invent expletives that mean nothing bad? As if Mr. Rampant were to say, 'Cockatoos and kingfishers! where are my shooting-boots?' For you know I do think it would make him more comfortable to put it in that way, especially if he had been kept waiting for them."

I paused, and Aunt Isobel turned round.

"Let us carry your idea well forward, Isobel. Bootjacks and expletives would no doubt be a relief to the thrower when hurled at servants or some one who could not (or from principle would not) retaliate, and the angry feelings that propelled them might be shortened by 'letting off the steam,' so to speak. But imagine yourself to have thrown a bootjack at Philip to relieve your feelings, and Philip (to relieve his) flinging it back at you. This would only give fresh impetus to *your* indignation, and whatever you threw next would not be likely to soothe *his*."

"Please don't!" said I. "Aunt Isobel, I could never throw a hatchet again."

"You are bold to promise to stop short anywhere when relieving passionate feelings by indulgence has begun on two sides. And, my dear, matters are no better where the indulgence is in words instead of blows. In the very mean and undignified position of abusing those who cannot return your abuse it might answer; but 'innocent strong language' would cease to be of any good when it was returned. If to 'Cockatoos and kingfishers! where are my shooting-boots?' an equally violent voice from below replied, 'Bats and blackbeetles! look for them yourself!' some stronger vent for the steam of hot temper would have to be found, and words of any kind would soon cease to relieve the feelings. Isobel, I have had long and hard experience, and your ideas are not new ones to me. Believe me, child, the only real relief is in absolute conquest, and the earlier the battle begins, the easier and the shorter it will be. If one can keep irritability under, one may escape a struggle to the death with passion. I am not cramming principles down your throat—I say as a matter of personal practice, that I do not know, and never hope to find a smoother or a shorter way. But I can say also—after Victory comes Peace."

I gave a heavy sigh.

"Thank you, Aunt Isobel, I will try; but it makes my second difficulty all the worse. I can fancy that I might possibly learn self-control; I can fancy by main force holding my tongue, or compelling it to speak very slowly and civilly: but one can't force one's feelings. Aunt Isobel, if I had been very much insulted or provoked, I might keep on being civil for years on the outside, but how I should hate! You can't prevent yourself hating. People talk about 'forgive and forget.' If forgiving means doing no harm, and forgetting means behaving quite civilly, as if nothing had happened, one could. But of course it's nonsense to talk of making yourself really *forget* anything. And I think it's just as absurd to talk of making yourself forgive, if forgiveness means feeling really kindly and comfortable as you did before. The very case in which I am most sure you are right about self-control is one of the worst the other way. I ought to be ashamed to speak of it—but I mean the hatchet-quarrel. If I had been very good instead of very wicked, and had restrained myself when Philip pulled all my work to pieces, and jeered at me for being miserable, I *couldn't* have loved him again as I did before. Forgive and forget! One would often be very glad to. I have often awoke in the morning and known that I had forgotten something disagreeable, and when it did come back I was sorry; but one's memory isn't made of slate, or one's heart either, that one can take a wet sponge and make it clean. Oh dear! I wonder why ill-tempered people are allowed to live! They ought to be smothered in their cradles."

Aunt Isobel was about to reply, but I interrupted her.

"Don't think me humble-minded, Aunt Isobel, for I'm not. Sometimes I feel inclined to think that ill-tempered people have more sense of justice and of the strict rights and wrongs of things—at least if they are not very bad," I interpolated, thinking of Mr. Rampant—"than people who can smile and look pleasant at everything and everybody like Lucy Lambent, who goes on calling me darling when I know I'm scowling like a horned-owl. Nurse says she's the 'sweetest tempered young lady she ever did know!' Aunt Isobel, what a muddle life is!"

"After some years of it," said my aunt, pulling her lashes hard, "*I* generally say, What a muddle my head is! Life is too much for it."

"I am quite willing to put it that way," sighed I, laying my muddle-head on the table, for I was tired. "It comes to much the same thing. Now—there is my great difficulty! I give in about the other one, but you can't cure this, and the truth is, I am not fit to go to a confirmation-class, much less to the Holy Communion."

"Isobel," said my aunt, folding her hands on her lap, and bending her very thick brows on the fire, "I want you to clearly understand that I speak with great hesitation, and without any authority. I can do nothing for you but tell you what I have found myself in *my* struggles."

"Thank you a thousand times," said I, "that's what I want. You know I hear two sermons every Sunday, and I have a lot of good books. Mrs. Welment sends me a little book about ill-temper every Christmas. The last one was about saying a little hymn before you let yourself speak whenever you feel angry. Philip got hold of it, and made fun of it. He said it was like the recipe for catching a sparrow by putting salt on its tail, because if you were cool enough to say a hymn, there would then be no need for saying it. What do you think, Aunt Isobel?"

"My dear, I have long ago given up the idea that everybody's weak points can all be strengthened by one plaster. The hymn might be very useful in some cases, though I confess that it would not be in mine. But prayer is; and I find a form of prayer necessary. At the same time I have such an irritable taste, that there are very few forms of devotion that give me much help but the Prayer-Book collects and Jeremy Taylor. I do not know if you may find it useful to hear that in this struggle I sometimes find prayers more useful, if they are not too much to the sore point. A prayer about ill-temper might tend to make me cross, when the effort to join my spirit with the temptation-tried souls of all ages in a solemn prayer for the Church Universal would lift me out of the petty sphere of personal vexations, better than going into my grievances even piously. I speak merely of myself, mind."

"Thank you," I said. "But about what I said about hating. Aunt Isobel, did you ever change your feelings by force? Do you suppose anybody ever did?"

"I believe it is a great mistake to trouble one's self with the spiritual experiences of other people when one cannot fully know their circumstances, so I won't suppose at all. As to what I am sure of, Isobel, you know I speak the truth."

"Yes," said I; it would have been impertinence to say more.

"*I* have found that if one fights for good behaviour, GOD makes one a present of the good feelings. I believe you will find it so. Even when you were a child, if you had tried to be good, and had managed to control yourself, and had not thrown the hatchet, I am quite sure you would not have hated Philip for long. Perhaps you would have thought how much better Philip used to behave before your father and mother died, and a little elder-sisterly, motherly feeling would have mixed with your wrath at seeing him with his fat legs planted apart, and his shoulders up, the very picture of wilful naughtiness. Perhaps you might have thought you had repulsed him a little harshly when he wanted to help, as you were his chief playmate and twin sister."

"Please don't," said I. "How I wish I had! Indeed I don't know how I can ever speak of hating one of the others when there are so few of us, and we are orphans. But everybody isn't one's brother. And—oh, Aunt Isobel, at the time one does get so wild, and hard, and twisted in one's heart!"

"I don't think it is possible to overrate the hardness of the first close struggle with any natural passion," said my aunt earnestly; "but indeed the easiness of after-steps is often quite beyond one's expectations. The free gift of grace with which GOD perfects our efforts may come in many ways, but I am convinced that it is the common experience of Christians that it does come."

"To every one, do you think?" said I. "I've no doubt it comes to you, Aunt Isobel, but then you are so good."

"For pity's sake don't say I am good," said my aunt, and she kicked down all the fire-irons; and then begged my pardon, and picked them up again.

We were silent for awhile. Aunt Isobel sat upright with her hands folded in her lap, and that look which her large eyes wear when she is trying to see all the sides of a question. They were dilated with a sorrowful earnestness when she spoke again.

"There *may* be some souls," she said, "whose brave and bitter lot it is to conquer comfortless. Perhaps some terrible inheritance of strong sin from the father is visited upon the son, and, only able to keep his purpose pure, he falls as fast as he struggles up, and still struggling falls again. Soft moments of peace with GOD and man may never come to him. He may feel himself viler than a thousand trumpery souls who could not have borne his trials for a day. Child, for you and for me is reserved no such cross and no such crown as theirs who falling still fight, and fighting fall, with their faces Zionwards, into the arms of the Everlasting Father. 'As one whom his mother comforteth' shall be the healing of *their* wounds."

There was a brisk knock at the door, and Philip burst in.

"Look here, Isobel, if you mean to be late for confirmation-class I'm not going to wait for you. I hate sneaking in with the benches all full, and old Bartram blinking and keeping your place in the catechism for you with his fat forefinger."

"I am *very* sorry, Philip dear," said I; "please go without me, and I'll come on as quickly as I can. Thank you very much for coming to remind me."

"There's no such awful hurry," said Philip in a mollified tone; "I'll wait for you down-stairs."

Which he did, whistling.

Aunt Isobel and I are not demonstrative, it does not suit us. She took hold of my arms, and I laid my head on her shoulder.

"Aunt Isobel, GOD help me, I will fight on to the very end."

"HE *will* help you," said Aunt Isobel.

I could not look at her face and doubt it. Oh, my weak soul, never doubt it more!

CHAPTER V

CELESTIAL FIRE—I CHOOSE A TEXT

We were confirmed.

As Aunt Isobel had said, I was spared perplexity by the unmistakable nature of my weakest point. There was no doubt as to what I should pray against and strive against. But on that day it seemed not only as if I could never give way to ill-temper again, but as if the trumpery causes of former outbreaks could never even tempt me to do so. As the lines of that ancient hymn to the Holy Ghost—"*Veni Creator*"—rolled on, I prayed humbly enough that my unworthy efforts might yet be crowned by the sevenfold gifts of the Spirit; but that a soul which sincerely longed to be "lightened with celestial fire" could be tempted to a common fit of sulks or scolding by the rub of nursery misdeeds and mischances, felt then so little likely as hardly to be worth deprecating on my knees.

And yet, when the service was over, the fatigue of the mental strain and of long kneeling and standing began to tell in a feeling that came sadly near to peevishness. I spent the rest of the day resolutely in my room and on my knees, hoping to keep up those high thoughts and emotions which had made me feel happy as well as good. And yet I all but utterly broke down into the most commonplace crossness because Philip did not do as I did, but romped noisily with the others, and teased me for looking grave at tea.

I just did not break down. So much remained alive of the "celestial fire," that I kept my temper behind my teeth. Long afterwards, when I learnt by accident that Philip's "good resolve" on the occasion had been that he would be kinder to "the little ones," I was very glad that I had not indulged my uncharitable impulse to lecture him on indifference to spiritual progress.

That evening Aunt Isobel gave me a new picture for my room. It was a fine print of the Crucifixion, for which I had often longed, a German woodcut in the powerful manner of Albert Duerer, after a design by Michael Angelo. It was neither too realistic nor too mediaeval, and the face was very noble. Aunt Isobel had had it framed, and below on an illuminated scroll was written—"What are these wounds in Thine Hands? Those with which I was wounded in the house of My friends."

"I often think," she said, when we had hung it up and were looking at it, "that it is not in our Lord's Cross and Passion that His patience comes most home to us. To be patient before an unjust judge or brutal soldiers might be almost a part of self-respect; but patience with the daily disappointments of a life 'too good for this world,' as people say, patience with the follies, the unworthiness, the ingratitude of those one loves—these things are our daily example. For wounds in the house of our enemies pride may be prepared; wounds in the house of our friends take human nature by surprise, and GOD only can teach us to bear them. And with all reverence I think that we may say that ours have an element of difficulty in which His were wanting. They are mixed with blame on our own parts."

"That is why you have put that text for me?" said I. My aunt nodded.

I was learning to illuminate, and I took much pride in my room. I determined to make a text for myself, and to choose a very plain passage about ill-temper. Mrs. Welment's books supplied me with plenty. I chose "Let not the sun go down upon your wrath," but I resolved to have the complete text as it stands in the Bible. It seemed fair to allow myself to remember that anger is not always a sin, and I thought it useful to remind myself that if by obstinate ill-temper I got the victory in a quarrel, it was only because the devil had got the victory over me. So the text ran full length:—"Be ye angry, and sin not; let not the sun go down upon your wrath: neither give place to the devil." It made a very long scroll, and I put it up over my window, and fastened it with drawing-pins.

CHAPTER VI

THEATRICAL PROPERTIES—I PREPARE A PLAY—PHILIP BEGINS TO PREPARE THE SCENERY—A NEW FRIEND

Philip was at school during the remainder of the year, but I tried to put my good resolves in practice with the children, and it made us a more peaceful household than usual. When Philip came home for the Christmas holidays we were certainly in very pleasant moods—for an ill-tempered family.

Our friends allow that some quickness of wits accompanies the quickness of our tempers. From the days when we were very young our private theatricals have been famous in our own little neighbourhood. I was paramount in nursery mummeries, and in the children's charade parties of the district, for Philip was not very reliable when steady help was needed; but at school he became stage-manager of the theatricals there.

I do not know that he learned to act very much better than I, and I think Alice (who was only twelve) had twice the gift of either of us, but every half he came back more ingenious than before in matters for which we had neither the talent nor the tools. He glued together yards of canvas or calico, and produced scenes and drop-curtains which were ambitious and effective, though I thought him a little reckless both about good drawing and good clothes. His glue-kettles and size-pots were always steaming, his paint was on many and more inappropriate objects than the canvas. A shilling's-worth of gilding powder went such a long way that we had not only golden crowns and golden sceptres, and golden chains for our dungeon, and golden wings for our fairies, but the nursery furniture became irregularly and unintentionally gilded, as well as nurse's stuff dress, when she sat on a warrior's shield, which was drying in the rocking-chair.

But these were small matters. Philip gave us a wonderful account of the "properties" he had made for school theatricals. A dragon painted to the life, and with matches so fixed into the tip of him that the boy who acted as the life and soul of this ungainly carcase could wag a fiery tail before the amazed audience, by striking it on that particular scale of his dragon's skin which was made of sand-paper. Rabbit-skin masks, cotton-wool wigs and wigs of tow, seven-league boots, and witches' hats, thunder with a tea-tray, and all the phases of the moon with a moderator lamp—with all these things Philip enriched the school theatre, though for some time he would not take so much trouble for our own.

But during this last half he had written me three letters—and three very kind ones. In the latest he said that—partly because he had been making some things for us, and partly because of changes in the school-theatrical affairs—he should bring home with him a box of very valuable "properties" for our use at Christmas. He charged me at once to prepare a piece which should include a prince disguised as a woolly beast on two legs with large fore-paws (easily shaken off), a fairy godmother with a tow wig and the highest hat I could ever hope to see, a princess turned into a willow-tree (painted from memory of the old one at home), and with fine gnarls and knots, through which the princess could see everything, and prompt (if needful), a disconsolate parent, and a faithful attendant, to be acted by one person, with as many belated travellers as the same actor could personate into the bargain. These would all be eaten up by the dragon at the right wing, and re-enter more belated than ever at the left, without stopping longer than was required to roll a peal of thunder at the back. The fifth and last character was to be the dragon himself. The forest scene would be wanted, and I was to try and get an old cask for a cave.

I must explain that I was not expected to write a play. We never took the trouble to "learn parts." We generally took some story which pleased us out of *Grimm's Fairy Tales* or the *Arabian Nights*, and arranged for the various scenes. We each had a copy of the arrangement, and our proper characters were assigned to us. After this we did the dialogue as if it had been a charade. We were well accustomed to act together, and could trust each other and ourselves. Only Alice's brilliancy ever took us by surprise.

By the time that Philip came home I had got in the rough outline of the plot. He arrived with a box of properties, the mere size of which raised a cheer of welcome from the little ones, and red-hot for our theatricals.

Philip was a little apt to be red-hot over projects, and to cool before they were accomplished; but on this occasion we had no forebodings of such evil. Besides, he was to play the dragon! When he did fairly devote himself to anything, he grudged no trouble and hesitated at no undertakings. He was so much pleased with my plot and with the cave, that he announced that he should paint a new forest scene for the occasion. I tried to dissuade him. There were so many other things to be done, and the old scene was very good. But he had learnt several new tricks of the scene-painter's trade, and was bent upon putting them into practice. So he began his new scene, and I resolved to work all the harder at the odds and ends of our preparations. To be driven into a corner and pressed for time always stimulated instead of confusing me. I think the excitement of it is pleasant. Alice had the same dogged way of working at a crisis, and we felt quite confident of being able to finish up "at a push," whatever Philip might leave undone. The theatricals were to be on Twelfth Night.

Christmas passed very happily on the whole. I found my temper much oftener tried since Philip's return, but this was not only because he was very wilful and very fond of teasing, but because with the younger ones I was always deferred to.

One morning we were very busy in the nursery, which was our workshop. Philip's glue-pots and size-pots were steaming, there were coloured powders on every chair, Alice and I were laying a coat of invisible green over the cave-cask, and Philip, in radiant good-humour, was giving distance to his woodland glades in the most artful manner with powder-blue, and calling on us for approbation—when the housemaid came in.

"It's *not* lunch-time?" cried Alice. "It can't be!"

"Get away, Mary," said Philip, "and tell cook if she puts on any more meals I'll paint her best cap pea-green. She's sending up luncheons and dinners all day long now: just because she knows we're busy."

Mary only laughed, and said, "It's a gentleman wants to see you, Master Philip," and she gave him a card. Philip read it, and we waited with some curiosity.

"It's a man I met in the train," said he, "a capital fellow. He lives in the town. His father's a doctor there. Granny must invite him to the theatricals. Ask him to come here, Mary, and show him the way."

"Oughtn't you to go and fetch him yourself?" said I.

"I can't leave this," said Philip. "He'll be all right. He's as friendly as possible."

I must say here that "Granny" was our maternal grandmother, with whom we lived. My mother and father were cousins, and Granny's husband was of that impetuous race to which we belonged. If he had been alive he would have kept us all in good order, no doubt. But he was dead, and Granny was the gentlest of old ladies: I fear she led a terrible life with us all!

Philip's friend came up-stairs. He *was* very friendly; in fact Alice and I thought him forward, but he was several years older than Philip, who seemed proud of the acquaintance. Perhaps Alice and I were biased by the fact that he spoilt our pleasant morning. He was one of those people who look at everything one has been working at with such unintelligent eyes that their indifference ought not to dishearten one; and yet it does.

"It's for our private theatricals," said Philip, as Mr. Clinton's amazed stare passed from our paint-covered selves to the new scene.

"My cousins in Dublin have private theatricals," said Mr. Clinton. "My uncle has built on a room for the theatre. All the fittings and scenes come from London, and the first costumiers in Dublin send in all the dresses and everything that is required on the afternoon before the performance."

"Oh, we're in a much smaller way," said Philip; "but I've some properties here that don't look bad by candlelight." But Mr. Clinton had come up to the cask, and was staring at it and us. I knew by the way Alice got quietly up, and shook some chips with a decided air out of her apron, that she did not like being stared at. But her movement only drew Mr. Clinton's especial attention.

"You'll catch it from your grandmamma for making such a mess of your clothes, won't you?" he asked.

"I *beg* your pardon?" said Alice, with so perfect an air of not having heard him that he was about to repeat the question, when she left the nursery with the exact exit which she had made as a Discreet Princess repelling unwelcome advances in last year's play.

I was afraid of an outburst from Philip, and said in hasty civility, "This is a cave we are making."

"They'd a splendid cave at Covent Garden last Christmas," said Mr. Clinton. "It covered half the stage. An enormously tall man dressed in cloth of silver stood in the entrance, and waved a spear ten or twelve feet long over his head. A fairy was let down above that, so you may be sure the cave was pretty big."

"Oh, here's the dragon," said Philip, who had been rummaging in the property box. "He's got a fiery tail."

"They were quite the go in pantomimes a few years ago," said Mr. Clinton, yawning. "My uncle had two or three— bigger than that, of course."

Philip saw that his friend was not interested in amateur property-making, and changed the subject.

"What have you been doing this morning?" said he.

"I drove here with my father, who had got to pass your gates. I say, there's splendid shooting on the marsh now. I want you to come out with me, and we'll pot a wild duck or two."

"I've no gun," said Philip, and to soften the statement added, "there's no one here to go out with."

"I'll go out with you. And I say, we could just catch the train back to the town, and if you'll come and lunch with us, we'll go out a bit this afternoon and look round. But you must get a gun."

"I should like some fresh air," said Philip, "and as you've come over for me—"

I knew the appealing tone in his voice was for my ears, for my face had fallen.

"Could I be going on with it?" I asked, nodding towards the forest scene.

"Oh dear no! I'll go at it again to-night. It ought all to be painted by candlelight by rights. I'm not going to desert my post," he added.

"I hope not," said I as good-humouredly as I could; but dismay was in my heart.

CHAPTER VII

A QUARREL—BOBBY IS WILLING—EXIT PHILIP

Philip came back by an evening train, and when he had had something to eat he came up to the nursery to go on with the scene. We had got everything ready for him, and he worked for about half-an-hour. But he was so sleepy, with cold air and exercise, that he did not paint well, and then he got impatient, and threw it up—"till the morning."

In the morning he set to work, talking all the time about wild duck and teal, and the price of guns; but by the time he had put last night's blunders straight, the front door bell rang, and Mary announced "Mr. Clinton."

Philip was closeted in his room with his new friend till twelve o'clock. Then they went out into the yard, and finally Mr. Clinton stayed to luncheon. But I held my peace, and made Alice hold hers. Mr. Clinton went away in the afternoon, but Philip got the plate-powder and wash-leather, and occupied himself in polishing the silver fittings of his dressing-case.

"I think you might do that another time, Philip," said I; "you've not been half-an-hour at the properties to-day, and you could clean your bottles and things quite as well after the theatricals."

"As it happens I just couldn't," said Philip; "I've made a bargain, and bargains won't wait."

Alice and I screamed in one breath, "You're *not* going to give away the dressing-case!"—for it had been my father's.

"I said a *bargain*" replied Philip, rubbing harder than ever; "you can't get hold of a gun every day Without paying down hard cash."

"I hate Mr. Clinton!" said Alice.

It was a very unfortunate speech, for it declared open war; and when this is done it cannot be undone. There is no taking back those sharp sayings which the family curse hangs on the tips of our tongues.

Philip and Alice exchanged them pretty freely. Philip called us selfish, inhospitable, and jealous. He said we grudged his enjoying himself in the holidays, when he had been working like a slave for us during the half. That we disliked his friend because he *was* his friend, and (not to omit the taunt of sex) that Clinton was too manly a fellow to please girls, etc., etc. In self-defence Alice was much more out-spoken about both Philip and Mr. Clinton than she had probably intended to be. That Philip began things hotly, and that his zeal cooled before they were accomplished—that his imperiousness laid him open to flattery, and the necessity of playing first-fiddle betrayed him into second-rate friendships, which were thrown after the discarded hobbies—that Mr. Clinton was ill-bred, and with that vulgarity of mind which would make him rather proud than ashamed of getting the best of a bargain with his friend—these things were not the less taunts because they were true.

If the violent scenes which occur in ill-tempered families *felt* half as undignified and miserable as they *look*, surely they would be less common! I believe Philip and Alice would have come to blows if I had not joined with him to expel her from the room. I was not happy about it, for my sympathy was on her side of the quarrel, but she had been the one to declare war, and I could not control Philip. In short, it is often not easy to keep the peace and be just too, as I should like to have said to Aunt Isobel, if she had been at home. But she was to be away until the 6th.

Alice defeated, I took Philip seriously to task. Not about his friend—the subject was too sore, and Alice had told him all that we thought, and rather more than we thought on that score—but about the theatricals. I said if he really was tired of the business we would throw it up, and let our friends know that the proposed entertainment had fallen through, but that if he wanted it to go forward he must decide what help he would give, and then abide by his promise.

We came to terms. If I would let him have a day or two's fun with his gun, Philip promised to "spurt," as he called it, at the end. I told him we would be content if he would join in a "thorough rehearsal," the afternoon before, and devote himself to the business on the day of the performance.

"Real business, you know," I added, "with nobody but ourselves. Nobody coming in to interrupt."

"Of course," said Philip; "but I'll do more than that, Isobel. There's the scene—"

"*We'll* finish the scene," said I, "if you don't aggravate Alice so that I lose her help as well as yours."

Alice was very sulky, which I could hardly wonder at, and I worked alone, except for Bobby, the only one with anything

Juliana Horatia Ewing

like a good temper among us, who roasted himself very patiently with my size-pot, and hammered bits of ivy, and of his fingers, rather neatly over the cave. But Alice was impulsive and kind-hearted. When I got a bad headache, from working too long, she came round, and helped me. Philip was always going to do so, but as a matter of fact he went out every day with the old fowling-piece for which he had given his dressing case.

When the ice bore Charles also deserted us, but Alice and I worked steadily on at dresses and scenery. And Bobby worked with us.

The 5th of January arrived, the day before the theatricals. Philip spent the morning in cleaning his gun, and after luncheon he brought it into the nursery to "finish" with a peculiarly aggravating air.

"When shall you be ready to rehearse?" I asked.

"Oh, presently," said Philip, "there's plenty of time yet. It's a great nuisance," he added, "I'll never have anything to do with theatricals again. They make a perfect slave of one."

"*You've* not slaved much, at any rate," said Charles.

"You'd better not give me any of your cheek," said Philip threateningly.

"We've done without him for a week, I don't know why we shouldn't do without him to-morrow," muttered Alice from the corner where she was sewing gold paper stars on to the Enchanted Prince's tunic.

"I wish you could," growled Philip, who took the suggestion more quietly than I expected; "anybody could do the Dragon, there's no acting in it!"

"I won't," said Charles, "Isobel gave me the Enchanted Prince or the Woolly Beast, and I shall stick to my part."

"Could I do the Dragon?" asked Bobby, releasing his hot face from the folds of an old blue cloak lined with red, in which he was rehearsing his walk as a belated wayfarer.

"Certainly not," said I, "you're the Bereaved Father and the Faithful Attendant to begin with, and I hope you won't muddle them. And you're Twelve Travellers as well, and the thunder, remember!"

"I don't care how many I do, if only I can," said Bobby, drawing his willing arm across his steaming forehead. "I should like to have a fiery tail."

"You can't devour yourself once—let alone twelve times," said I sternly. "Don't be silly, Bob."

It was not Bob I was impatient with in reality, it was Philip.

"If you really mean to desert the theatricals after all you promised, I would much rather try to do without you," said I indignantly.

"Then you may!" retorted Philip. "I wash my hands of it and of the whole lot of you, and of every nursery entertainment henceforward!" and he got the fragments of his gun together with much clatter. But Charles had posted himself by the door to say his say, and to be ready to escape when he had said it.

"You're ashamed of it, that's it," said he; "you want to sit among the grown-ups with a spy-glass, now you've got

Apothecary Clinton's son for a friend,"—and after this brief and insulting summary of the facts, Charles vanished. But Philip, white with anger, was too quick for him, and at the top of the back-stairs he dealt him such a heavy blow that Charles fell head-long down the first flight.

Alice and I flew to the rescue. I lived in dread of Philip really injuring Charles some day, for his blows were becoming serious ones as he grew taller and stronger, and his self-control did not seem to wax in proportion. And Charles's temper was becoming very aggressive. On this occasion, as soon as he had regained breath, and we found that no bones were broken, it was only by main force that we held him back from pursuing Philip.

"I'll hit him—I'll stick to him," he sobbed in his fury, shaking his head like a terrier, and doubling his fists. But he was rather sick with the fall, and we made him lie down to recover himself, whilst Alice, Bobby, and I laid our heads together to plan a substitute for Philip in the Dragon.

When bed-time came, and Philip was still absent, we became uneasy, and as I lay sleepless that night I asked myself if I had been to blame for the sulks in which he had gone off. In fits of passion Philip had often threatened to go away and never let us hear of him again. I knew that such things did happen, and it made me unhappy when he went off like this, although his threats had hitherto been no more than a common and rather unfair device of ill-temper.

CHAPTER VIII

I HEAR FROM PHILIP—A NEW PART WANTED—I LOSE MY TEMPER—WE ALL LOSE OUR TEMPERS

Next morning's post brought the following letter from Philip:—

"MY DEAR ISOBEL,

"You need not bother about the Dragon—I'll do it. But I wish you would put another character into the piece. It is for Clinton. He says he will act with us. He says he can do anything if it is a leading part. He has got black velvet knickerbockers and scarlet stockings, and he can have the tunic and cloak I wore last year, and the flap hat; and you must lend him your white ostrich feather. Make him some kind of a grandee. If you can't, he must be the Prince, and Charles can do some of the Travellers. We are going out on the marsh this morning, but I shall be with you after luncheon, and Clinton in the evening. He does not want any rehearsing, only a copy of the plan. Let Alice make it, her writing is the clearest, and I wish she would make me a new one; I've torn mine, and it is so dirty, I shall never be able to read it inside the Dragon. Don't forget.

"Your affectionate brother, "PHILIP."

There are limits to one's patience, and with some of us they are not very wide. Philip had passed the bounds of mine, and my natural indignation was heightened by a sort of revulsion from last night's anxiety on his account. His lordly indifference to other people's feelings was more irritating than the trouble he gave us by changing his mind.

"You won't let him take the Woolly Beast from me, Isobel?" cried Charles. "And you know you promised to lend *me* your ostrich plume."

"Certainly not," said I. "And you shall have the feather. I promised."

"If Mr. Clinton acts—I shan't," said Alice.

"Mr. Clinton won't act," said I, "I can't alter the piece now. But I wish, Alice, you were not always so very ready to drive things into a quarrel."

"If we hadn't given way to Philip so much he wouldn't think we can bear anything," said Alice.

I could not but feel that there was some truth in this, and that it was a dilemma not provided against in Aunt Isobel's teaching, that one may be so obliging to those one lives with as to encourage, if not to teach them to be selfish.

Perhaps it would have been well if on the first day when Philip deserted us Alice and I, had spent the afternoon with Lucy Lambent, and if we had continued to amuse ourselves with our friends when Philip amused himself with his. We should then have been forced into a common decision as to whether the play should be given up, and, without reproaches or counter-reproaches, Philip would have learned that he could not leave all the work to us, and then arrange and disarrange the plot at his own pleasure, or rather, he would never have thought that he could. But a plan of this kind requires to be carried out with perfect coolness to be either justifiable or effective. And we have not a cool head amongst us.

One thing was clear. I ought to keep faith with the others who had worked when Philip would not. Charles should not be turned out of his part I rather hustled over the question of a new part for Mr. Clinton in my mind. I disliked him, and did not want to introduce him. I said to myself that it was quite unreasonable—out of the question in fact—and I prepared to say so to Philip.

Of course he was furious—that I knew he would be; but I was firm.

"Charles can be the Old Father, and the Family Servant too," said he. "They're both good parts."

"Then give them to Mr. Clinton," said I, well knowing that he would not. "Charles has taken a great deal of pains with his part, and these are his holidays as well as yours, and the Prince shall not be taken from him."

"Well, I say it shall. And Charles may be uncommonly glad if I let him act at all after the way he behaved yesterday."

"The way *you* behaved, you, mean," said I—for my temper was slipping from my grasp;—"you might have broken his neck."

"All the more danger in his provoking me, and in your encouraging him."

I began to feel giddy, which is always a bad sign with us. It rang in my mind's ear that this was what came of being

Juliana Horatia Ewing

forbearing with a bully like Philip. But I still tried to speak quietly.

"If you think," said I through my teeth, "that I am going to let you knock the others about, and rough-ride it over our theatricals, you are mistaken."

"*Your* theatricals!" cried Philip, mimicking me. "I like that! Whom do the properties belong to, pray?"

"If it goes by buying," was my reply to this rather difficult question, "most of them belong to Granny, for the canvas and the paints and the stuff for the dresses, have gone down in the bills; and if it goes by work, I think we have done quite as much as you. And if some of the properties *are* yours, the play is mine. And as to the scene—you did the distance in the middle of the wood, but Alice and I painted all the foreground."

"Then you may keep your foreground, and I'll take my distance," roared Philip, and in a moment his pocket-knife was open, and he had cut a hole a foot-and-a-half square in the centre of the Enchanted Forest, and Bobby's amazed face (he was running a tuck in his cloak behind the scenes) appeared through the aperture.

If a kind word would have saved the fruits of our week's hard labour, hot one of us would have spoken it. We sacrifice anything we possess in our ill-tempered family—except our wills.

"And you may take your play, and I'll take my properties," continued Philip, gathering up hats, wigs, and what not from the costumes which Alice and I had arranged in neat groups ready for the green-room. "I'll give everything to Clinton this evening for his new theatre, and we'll see how you get on without the Fiery Dragon."

"Clinton *can't* want a fiery dragon when he's got you," said Charles, in a voice of mock compliment.

The Fairy Godmother's crabstick was in Philip's hand. He raised it, and flew at Charles, but I threw myself between them and caught Philip's arm.

"You shall not hit him," I cried.

Aunt Isobel is right about one thing. If one *does* mean to stop short in a quarrel one must begin at a very early stage. It is easier to smother one's feelings than to check one's words. By the time it comes to blows it is like trying to pull up a runaway horse. The first pinch Philip gave to my arm set my brain on fire. When he threw me heavily against the cave with a mocking laugh, and sprang after Charles, I could not have yielded an inch to him to save my life—not to earn Fortunatus' purse, or three fairy wishes—not to save whatever I most valued.

What would have induced me? I do not know, but I know that I am very glad it is not quite so easy to sell one's soul at one bargain as fairy-tales make out!

My struggle with Philip had given Charles time to escape. Philip could not find him, and rough as were the words with which he returned to me, I fancy they cost him some effort of self-control, and they betrayed to Alice's instinct and mine that he would have been glad to get out of the extremity to which our tempers had driven matters.

"Look here!" said he in a tone which would have been perfect if we had been acting a costermonger and his wife. "Are you going to make Clinton the Prince or not?"

"I am not," said I, nursing my elbow, which was cut by a nail on the cask. "I am not going to do anything whatever for Mr. Clinton, and I ought to be cured of working for you."

"You have lost an opening to make peace," said an inner voice. "You've given the yielding plan a fair trial, and it has failed," said self-justification—the swiftest pleader I know. "There are some people, with self-satisfied, arbitrary tempers, upon whom gentleness is worse than wasted, because it misleads them. They have that remnant of savage notions which drives them to mistake generosity for weakness. The only way to convince them is to hit them harder than they hit you. And it is the kindest plan for everybody concerned."

I am bound to say—though it rather confuses some of my ideas—that experience has convinced me that this last statement is not without truth. But I am also bound to say that it was not really applicable to Philip. He is not as generous as Alice, but I had no good reason to believe that kindly concession would be wasted on him.

When I had flung my last defiance, Philip replied in violent words of a kind which girls in our class of life do not (happily!) use, even in a rage. They were partly drowned by the clatter with which he dragged his big box across the floor, and filled it with properties of all kinds, from the Dragon to the foot-light reflectors.

"I am going by the 4.15 to the town," said he, as he pulled the box out towards his own room. "You need not wait for either Clinton or me. Pray 'ring up' punctually!"

At this moment—having fully realized the downfall of the theatricals—Bobby burst into a howl of weeping. Alice scolded him for crying, and Charles reproached her for scolding him, on the score that her antipathy to Mr. Clinton had driven Philip to this extreme point of insult and ill-temper.

Charles's own conduct had been so far from soothing, that Alice had abundant material for retorts, and she was not likely to be a loser in the war of words. What she did say I did not hear, for by that time I had locked myself up in my own room.

CHAPTER IX

SELF-REPROACH—FAMILY DISCOMFORT— OUT ON THE MARSH—VICTORY

If I could have locked myself up anywhere else I should have preferred it. I would have justified my own part in the present family quarrel to Aunt Isobel herself, and yet I would rather not have been alone just now with the text I had made and pinned up, and with my new picture. However, there was nowhere else to go to.

A restless way I have of pacing up and down when I am in a rage, has often reminded me of the habits of the more ferocious of the wild beasts in the Zoological Gardens, and has not lessened my convictions on the subject of the family temper. For a few prowls up and down my den I managed to occupy my thoughts with fuming against Philip's behaviour, but as the first flush of anger began to cool, there was no keeping out of my head the painful reflections which the sight of my text, my picture, and my books suggested—the miserable contrast between my good resolves and the result.

"It only shows," I muttered to myself, in a voice about as amiable as the growlings of a panther, "it only shows that it is quite hopeless. We're an ill-tempered family—a hopelessly ill-tempered family; and to try to cure us is like patching the lungs of a consumptive family, I don't even wish that I *could* forgive Philip. He doesn't deserve it."

And then as I nursed the cut on my elbow, and recalled the long hours of work at the properties, the damaged scene, the rifling of the green-room, and Philip's desertion with the Dragon, his probable industry for Mr. Clinton's theatricals, and the way he had left us to face our own disappointed audience, fierce indignation got the upper hand once more.

"I don't care," I growled afresh; "if I have lost my temper, I believe I was right to lose it—at least, that no one could have been expected not to lose it, I will never beg his pardon for it, let Aunt Isobel say what she will. I should hate him ever after if I did, for the injustice of the thing. Pardon, indeed!"

I turned at the top of the room and paced back towards the window, towards the long illuminated text, and that

"—Noble face,
So sweet and full of grace,"

which bent unchangeable from the emblem of suffering and self-sacrifice.

I have a trick of talking to myself and to inanimate objects. I addressed myself now to the text and the picture.

"But if I don't," I continued, "if after being confirmed with Philip in the autumn, we come to just one of our old catastrophes in the very next holidays, as bad as ever, and spiting each other to the last—I shall take you all down to-morrow! I don't pretend to be able to persuade myself that black is white—like Mrs. Rampant; but I am not a hypocrite, I won't ornament my room with texts, and crosses, and pictures, and symbols of Eternal Patience, when I do not even mean to *try* to sacrifice myself, or to be patient."

It is curious how one's faith and practice hang together. I felt very doubtful whether it was even desirable that I should. Whether we did not misunderstand GOD'S will, in thinking that it is well that people in the right should ever sacrifice themselves for those who are in the wrong. I did not however hide from myself, that to say this was to unsay all my resolves about my besetting sin. I decided to take down my texts, pictures, and books, and grimly thought that I would frame a fine photograph Charles had given me of a lioness, and would make a new inscription, the motto of the old Highland Clan Chattan—with which our family is remotely connected—"*Touch not the cat but a glove.*"[1]

[Footnote 1: *Anglice* "without a glove."]

"Put on your gloves next time, Master Philip!" I thought. "I shall make no more of these feeble attempts to keep in my claws, which only tempt you to irritate me beyond endurance. We're an ill-tempered family, and you're not the most amiable member of it. For my own part, I can control my temper when it is not running away with me, and be fairly kind to the little ones, so long as they do what I tell them. But, at a crisis like this, I can no more yield to your unreasonable wishes, stifle my just anger, apologize for a little wrong to you who owe apologies for a big one, and pave the way to peace with my own broken will, than the leopard can change his spots."

"And yet—*if I could*!"

It broke from me almost like a cry, "If my besetting sin *is* a sin, if I have given way to it under provocation—if this moment is the very hardest of the battle, and the day is almost lost—and if now, even now, I could turn round and tread down this Satan under my feet. If this were to-morrow morning, and I had done it—O my soul, what triumph, what satisfaction in past prayers, what hope for the future!

"Then thou shouldest believe the old legends of sinners numbered with the saints, of tyrants taught to be gentle, of the unholy learning to be pure—for one believes with heartiness what he has experienced—then text and picture and cross should hang on, in spite of frailty, and in this sign shalt thou conquer."

One ought to be very thankful for the blessings of good health and strong nerves, but I sometimes wish I could cry more easily. I should not like to be like poor Mrs. Rampant, whose head or back is always aching, and whose nerves make me think of the strings of an Æolian harp, on which Mr. Rampant, like rude Boreas, is perpetually playing with the tones of his voice, the creak of his boots, and the bang of his doors. But her tears do relieve, if they exhaust her, and back-ache cannot be as bad as heart-ache—hot, dry heart-ache, or cold, hard heart-ache. I think if I could have cried I could have felt softer. As it was I began to wish that I could do what I felt sure that I could not.

If I dragged myself to Philip, and got out a few conciliatory words, I should break down in a worse fury than before if he sneered or rode the high horse, "as he probably would," thought I.

On my little carved Prayer-book shelf lay with other volumes a copy of A Kempis, which had belonged to my mother. Honesty had already whispered that if I deliberately gave up the fight with evil this must be banished with my texts and pictures. At the present moment a familiar passage came into my head:

"When one that was in great anxiety of mind, often wavering between fear and hope, did once humbly prostrate himself in prayer, and said, 'O if I knew that I should persevere!' he presently heard within him an answer from GOD, which said, 'If thou didst know it, what would'st thou do? Do what thou would'st do then, and thou shalt be safe.'"

Supposing I began to do right, and trusted the rest? I could try to speak to Philip, and it would be something even if I stopped short and ran away. Or if I could not drag my feet to him, I could take Aunt Isobel's advice, and pray. I might not be able to speak civilly to Philip, or even to pray about him in my present state of mental confusion, but I could repeat *some* prayer reverently. Would it not be better to start on the right road, even if I fell by the way?

I crossed the room in three strides to the place where I usually say my prayers. I knelt, and folded my hands, and shut my eyes, and began to recite the Te Deum in my head, trying to attend to it. I did attend pretty well, but it was mere attention, till I felt slightly softened at the verse—"Make them to be numbered with Thy saints in glory everlasting." For my young mother was very good, and I always think of her when the choir comes to that verse on Sundays.

"Vouchsafe, O Lord, to keep us this day without sin." "It's too late to ask that," thought I, with that half of my brain which was not attending to the words of the Te Deum, "and yet there is a little bit of the day left which will be dedicated either to good or evil."

I prayed the rest, "O Lord, have mercy upon us, have mercy upon us. O Lord, let Thy mercy lighten upon us, as our trust is in Thee. O Lord, in Thee have I trusted, let me never be confounded!" and with the last verse there came from my heart a very passion of desire for strength to do the will of GOD at the sacrifice of my own. I flung myself on the floor with inarticulate prayers that were very fully to the point now, and they summed themselves up again in the old words, "In Thee, O Lord, have I trusted, let me never be confounded!"

When I raised my head I caught sight of the picture, and for an instant felt a superstitious thrill. The finely drawn face shone with a crimson glow. But in a moment more I saw the cause, and exclaimed—"*The sun is setting*! I must speak to Philip before it goes down."

What should I say? Somehow, now, my judgment felt very clear and decisive. I would not pretend that he had been in the right, but I would acknowledge where I had been in the wrong. I *had* been disobliging about Mr. Clinton, and I would say so, and offer to repair that matter. I would regret having lost my temper, and say nothing about his. I would not offer to deprive Charles of his part, or break my promise of the white feather; but I would make a new part for Mr. Clinton, and he should be quite welcome to any finery in my possession except Charles's plume. This concession was no difficulty to me. Bad as our tempers are, I am thankful to say they are not mean ones. If I dressed out Mr. Clinton at all, it would come natural to do it liberally. I would do all this—*if I could*. I might break down into passion at the mere sight of Philip and the properties, but at least I would begin "as if I knew I should persevere."

At this moment the front door was shut with a bang which shook the house.

It was Philip going to catch the 4.15. I bit my lips, and began to pull on my boots, watching the red sun as it sank over the waste of marshland which I could see from my window. I

Juliana Horatia Ewing

must try to overtake him, but I could run well, and I suspected that he would not walk fast. I did not believe that he was really pleased at the break-up of our plans and the prospect of a public exposure of our squabbles, though as a family we are always willing to make fools of ourselves rather than conciliate each other.

My things were soon on, and I hurried from my room. In the window-seat of the corridor was Alice. The sight of her reproached me. She slept in my room, but I jealously retained full power over it, and when I locked myself in she dared not disturb me.

"I'm afraid you've been wanting to come in," said I. "Do go in now."

"Thank you," said Alice, "I've nowhere to go to." Then tightening her lips, she added, "Philip's gone."

"I know," said I. "I'm going to try and get him back." Alice stared in amazement.

"You always do spoil Philip, because he's your twin," she said, at last; "you wouldn't do it for me."

"Oh, Alice, you don't know. I'd much rather do it for you, girls are so much less aggravating than boys. But don't try and make it harder for me to make peace."

"I beg your pardon, Isobel. If you do, you're an angel. I couldn't, to save my life."

At the head of the stairs I met Charles.

"He's gone," said he significantly, and bestriding the balustrades, he shot to the foot. When I reached him he was pinching the biceps muscle of his arm.

"Feel, Isobel," said he, "It's hard, isn't it?"

"Very, Charles, but I'm in a hurry."

"Look here," he continued, with an ugly expression on his face, "I'm going into training. I'm going to eat bits of raw mutton, and dumb-bell. Wait a year, wait half a year, and I shall be able to thrash him. I'll make him remember these theatricals. I don't forget. I haven't forgot his bursting my football out of spite."

It is not pleasant to see one's own sins reflected on other faces. I could not speak.

By the front door was Bobby. He was by way of looking out of the portico window, but his swollen eyes could not possibly have seen anything.

"Oh, Isobel, Isobel!" he sobbed, "Philip's gone, and taken the D—d—d—dragon with him, and we're all m—m—m—miserable."

"Don't cry, Bobby," said I, kissing him. "Finish your cloak, and be doing anything you can. I'm going to try and bring Philip back."

"Oh, thank you, thank you, Isobel! If only he'll come back I don't care what I do. Or I'll give up my parts if he wants them, and be a scene-shifter, if you'll lend me your carpet-slippers, and make me a paper cap."

"GOD has given you a very sweet temper, Bobby," said I, solemnly. "I wish I had one like it."

"You're as good as gold," said Bobby. His loving hug added strength to my resolutions, and I ran across the garden and jumped the ha-ha, and followed Philip over the marsh. I do not know whether he heard my steps when I came nearly up with him, but I fancy his pace slackened. Not that he looked round. He was much too sulky.

Philip is a very good-looking boy, much handsomer than I am, though we are alike. But the family curse disfigures his face when he is cross more than any one's, and the back view of him is almost worse than the front. His shoulders get so humped up, and his whole figure is stiff with cross-grained obstinacy.

"I shall never hold out if he speaks as ungraciously as he looks," thought I in despair. "But I'll not give in till I can hold out no longer."

"Philip!" I said. He turned round, and his face was no prettier to look at than his shoulders.

"What do you want?" (in the costermonger tone.)

"I want you to come back, Philip"—(here I choked).

"I dare say," he sneered, "and you want the properties! But you've got your play, and your amiable Charles, and your talented Alice, and your ubiquitous Bobby. And the audience will be entertained with an unexpected after-piece entitled— 'The disobliging disobliged.'"

Oh it *was* hard! I think if I had looked at Philip's face I must have broken down, but I kept my eyes steadily on the crimson sun, which loomed large through the marsh mists that lay upon the horizon, as I answered with justifiable vehemence:

"I have a very bad temper, Philip" (I checked the disposition to add—"and so have you"), "but I never tell a lie. I have *not* come after the properties. The only reason for which I have come is to try and make peace." At this point I gathered up all my strength and hurried on, staring at the sun till the bushes near us and the level waste of marsh beyond seemed to vanish in the glow. "I came to say that I am sorry for my share of the quarrel. I lost my temper, and I beg your pardon for that. I was not very obliging about Mr. Clinton, but you had tried me very much. However, what you did wrong, does not excuse me, I know, and if you like to come back, I'll make a new part as you wanted. I can't give him Charles's part, or the feather, but anything I can do, or give up of my own, I will. It's not because of to-night, for you know as well as I do that I do not care twopence what happens when I'm angry, and, after all, we can only say that you've taken the things. But I wanted us to get through these holidays without quarrelling, and I wanted you to enjoy them, and I want to try and be good to you, for you are my twin brother, and for my share of the quarrel I beg your pardon—I can do no more."

Some of this speech had been about as pleasant to say as eating cinders, and when it was done I felt a sudden sensation (very rare with me) of unendurable fatigue. As the last words left my lips the sun set, but my eyes were so bedazzled that I am not sure that I should not have fallen, but for an unexpected support. What Philip had been thinking of during my speech I do not know, for I had avoided looking at him, but when it was done he threw the properties out of his arms, and flung them around me with the hug of a Polar bear.

"You ill-tempered!" he roared. "You've the temper of an angel, or you would never have come after me like this. Isobel, I am a brute, I have behaved like a brute all the week,

and I beg *your* pardon."

I retract my wishes about crying, for when I do begin, I cry in such a very disagreeable way—no spring shower, but a perfect tempest of tears. Philip's unexpected generosity upset me, and I sobbed till I frightened him, and he said I was hysterical. The absurdity of this idea set me off into fits of laughing, which, oddly enough, seemed to distress him so much that I stopped at last, and found breath to say, "Then you'll come home?"

"If you'll have me. And never mind about Clinton, I'll get out of it. The truth is, Isobel, you and Alice did snub him from the first, and that vexed me; but I *am* disappointed in him. He does brag so, and I've had to take that fowling-piece to the gunsmith's already, so I know what it's worth. I did give Clinton a hint about it, and—would you believe it?—he laughed, and said he thought he had got the best of *that* bargain. I said, 'I hope you have, if it isn't an even one, for I should be very sorry to think *I* had cheated a friend!' But he either did not or wouldn't see it. He's a second-rate sort of fellow, I'm sure, and I'm sorry I promised to let him act. But I'll get out of it, you shan't be bothered by him."

"No, no," said I, "if you promised I'd much rather. It won't bother me at all."

(It is certainly a much pleasanter kind of dispute when the struggle is to give, and not to take!)

"You can't fit him in now?" said Philip doubtfully.

"Oh yes, I can." I felt sure that I could. I have often been short of temper for our amusements, but never of ideas. Philip tucked the properties under one arm, and me under the other, and as we ran homewards over the marsh, I threaded

Mr. Clinton into the plot with perfect ease.

"We'll have a second Prince, and he shall have an enchanted shield, which shall protect him from you—though he can't kill you—for Charles must do that. He shall be in love with the Princess too, but just when he and Charles are going to fight for her, the Fairy Godmother shall sprinkle him with the Waters of Memory, and break a spell which had made him forget his own Princess in a distant land. You know, Philip, if he *does* act well, he may make a capital part of it. It will be a splendid scene. We have two real metal swords, and as they are flashing in the air—enter the Fairy with the carved claret jug. When he is sprinkled he must drop his sword, and put his hands to his head. He will recall the picture of his own Princess, and draw it out and kiss it (I can lend him my locket miniature of great-grandpapa). Charles and he must swear eternal friendship, and then he will pick up his sword, and exit right centre, waving the golden shield, to find his Princess. It will look very well, and as he goes out the Princess can enter left in distraction about the combat, and she and Charles can fall in each other's arms, and be blessed by the Fairy."

"Capital!" said Philip. "What a head you have! But you're out of breath? We're running too fast."

"Not a bit," said I, "it refreshes me. Do you remember when you and I used to run hand in hand from the top to the bottom of Breakneck Hill? Oh, Philip, I do wish we could never quarrel any more! I think we might keep our tempers if we tried."

"*You* might," said Philip, "because you are good. But I shall always be a brute."

(Just what *I* said to Aunt Isobel! Must every one learn his own lessons for himself? I had a sort of unreasonable feeling that my experience ought to serve for the rest of our ill-tempered family into the bargain.)

Philip's spirits rose higher and higher. Of course he was delighted to be out of the scrape. I am sure he was glad to be friendly again, and he was hotter than ever for the theatricals.

So was I. I felt certain that they would be successful now. But far above and beyond the comfort of things "coming right," and the pleasure of anticipated fun, my heart was rocked to a higher peace. In my small religious experiences I had never known this triumph, this thankfulness before. Circumstances, not self-control, had helped me out of previous quarrels; I had never really done battle, and gained a conquest over my besetting sin. Now, however imperfectly and awkwardly, I yet *had* fought. If Philip had been less generous I might have failed, but the effort had been real—and it had been successful. Henceforth my soul should fight with the prestige of victory, with the courage that comes of having striven and won, trusted and not been confounded.

The first person we met after we got in was Aunt Isobel. She had arrived in our absence. No doubt she had heard the whole affair, but she is very good, and never *gauche* and she only said—

"Here come the stage-managers! Now what can I do to help? I have had some tea, and am ready to obey orders till the curtain rings up."

Boys do not carry things off well. Philip got very red, but I said—"Oh, please come to the nursery, Aunt Isobel. There are lots of things to do." She came, and was invaluable. I never said anything about the row to her, and she never said anything to me. That is what I call a friend!

The first thing Philip did was to unlock the property-box in his room and bring the Dragon and things back. The second thing he did was to mend the new scene by replacing the bit he had cut out, glueing canvas on behind it, and touching up with paint where it joined.

We soon put straight what had been disarranged. Blinds were drawn, candles lighted, seats fixed, and the theatre began to look like itself. Aunt Isobel and I were bringing in the footlights, when we saw Bobby at the extreme right of the stage wrapped in his cloak, and contemplating, with apparent satisfaction, twelve old hats and six pasteboard bandboxes which were spread before him.

"My dear Bobby, what are these?" said Aunt Isobel. Bobby hastily—almost stammeringly—explained,

"I am Twelve Travellers, you know, Aunt Isobel."

"Dear me!" said Aunt Isobel.

"I'll show you how I am going to do it," said Bobby.

"Here are twelve old hats—I have had such work to collect them!—and six bandboxes."

"Only six?" said Aunt Isobel with commendable gravity.

"But there are the lids," said Bobby; "six of them, and six boxes, make twelve, you know. I've only one cloak, but it's red on one side and blue on the other, and two kinds of buttons. Well; I come on left for the First Traveller, with my cloak the red side out, and this white chimney-pot hat."

"Ah!" said Aunt Isobel.

"And one of the bandboxes under my cloak. The Dragon attacks me in the centre, and drives me off the right, where I smash up the bandbox, which sounds like him crunching my bones. Then I roll the thunder, turn my cloak to the blue side, put on this wideawake, and come on again with a bandbox lid and crunch that, and roll more thunder, and so on. I'm the Faithful Attendant and the Bereaved Father as well," added Bobby, with justifiable pride, "and I would have done the Dragon if they would have let me."

But even Bobby did not outdo the rest of us in willingness. Alice's efforts were obvious tokens of remorse; she waited on Philip, was attentive to Mr. Clinton (who, I think, to this day believes that he made himself especially acceptable to "the young ladies"), and surpassed herself on the stage. Charles does not "come round" so quickly, but at the last moment he came and offered to yield the white plume. I confess I was rather vexed with Mr. Clinton for accepting it, but Alice and I despoiled our best hats of their black ostrich feathers to make it up to Charles, and he said, with some dignity, that he should never have offered the white one if he had not meant it to be accepted.

One thing took us by surprise. We had had more trouble over the dressing of the new Prince than the costumes and make-up of all the rest of the characters together cost—he was only just torn from the big looking-glass by his "call" to the stage, and, to our amazement, he seemed decidedly unwilling to go on.

"It's a very odd thing, Miss Alice," said he in accents so pitiable that I did not wonder that Alice did her best to encourage him,—"it's a most extraordinary thing, but I feel quite nervous."

"You'll be all right when you're once on," said Alice; "mind you don't forget that it depends on you to explain that it's an invincible shield."

"Which arm had I better wear it on?" said Mr. Clinton, shifting it nervously from side to side.

"The left, the left!" cried Alice. "Now you ought to be on."

"Oh what shall I say?" cried our new hero.

"Say—'Devastating Monster! my arm is mortal, and my sword was forged by human fingers, but this shield is invincible as—'"

"Second Prince," called Charles impatiently, and Mr. Clinton was hustled on.

He was greeted with loud applause. He said afterwards that this put his part out of his head, that Alice had told him wrong, and that the shield was too small for him.

As a matter of fact he hammered and stammered and got himself and the piece into such confusion, that Philip lost patience as he lay awaiting his cue. With a fierce bellow he emerged from his cask, and roaring, "Avaunt, knight of the invincible shield and craven heart!" he crossed the stage with the full clatter of his canvas joints, and chased Mr. Clinton off at the left centre.

Once behind the scenes, he refused to go on again. He said that he had never played without a proper part at his uncle's in Dublin, and thought our plan quite a mistake. Besides which, he had got toothache, and preferred to join the audience, which he did, and the play went on without him.

I was acting as stage-manager in the intervals of my part, when I noticed Mr. Clinton (not the ex-Prince, but his father, the surgeon) get up, and hastily leave his place among the spectators. But just as I was wondering at this, I was recalled to business by delay on the part of Bobby, who ought to have been on (with the lights down) as the Twelfth Traveller.

I found him at the left wing, with all the twelve hats fitted one over another, the whole pile resting on a chair.

"Bob, what are you after? You ought to be on."

"All right," said Bob, "Philip knows. He's lashing his tail and doing some business till I'm ready. Help me to put this cushion under my cloak for a hump-back, will you? I didn't like the twelfth hat, it's too like the third one, so I'm going on as a Jew Pedlar. Give me that box. Now!" And before I could speak a roar of applause had greeted Bobby as he limped on in his twelve hats, crying, "Oh tear, oh tear! dish ish the tarkest night I ever shaw."

But either we acted unusually well, or our audience was exceptionally kind, for it applauded everything and everybody till the curtain fell.

*　*　*　*　*

"Behind the scenes" is always a place of confusion after amateur theatricals; at least it used to be with us. We ran hither and thither, lost our every-day shoes, washed the paint from our faces, and mislaid any number of towels, and combs, and brushes, ate supper by snatches, congratulated ourselves on a successful evening, and were kissed all around by Granny, who came behind the scenes for the purpose.

All was over, and the guests were gone, when I gave an invitation to the others to come and make lemon-brew over my bedroom fire as an appropriate concluding festivity. (It had been suggested by Bobby.) I had not seen Philip for some time, but we were all astonished to hear that he had gone out. We kept his "brew" hot for him, and Charles and Bobby were both nodding—though they stoutly refused to go to bed,—when his step sounded in the corridor, and he knocked and came hastily in.

Everybody roused up.

"Oh, Philip, we've been wondering where you were! Here's your brew, and we've each kept a little drop, to drink your good health."

("Mine is *all* pips," observed Bobby as a parenthesis.) But Philip was evidently thinking of something else.

"Isobel," he said, standing by the table, as if he were making a speech, "I shall never forget your coming after me to-day. I told you you had the temper of an angel."

"So did I," said Alice.

"Hear! hear!" said Bobby, who was sucking his pips one by one and laying them by—"to plant in a pot," as he afterwards explained.

"You not only saved the theatricals," continued Philip, "you saved my life I believe."

No "situation" in the play had been half so startling as this. We remained open-mouthed and silent, whilst Philip sat down as if he were tired, and rested his head on his hands, which were dirty, and stained with something red.

"Haven't you heard about the accident?" he asked.

We all said "No."

"The 4.15 ran into the express where the lines cross, you know. Isobel, *there were only two first-class carriages, and everybody in them was killed but one man.* They have taken both his legs off, and he's not expected to live. Oh, poor fellow, he did groan so!"

Bobby burst into passionate tears, and Philip buried his head on his arms.

Neither Alice nor I could speak, but Charles got up and went round and stood by Philip.

"You've been helping," he said emphatically, "I know you have. You're a good fellow, Philip, and I beg your pardon for saucing you. I am going to forget about the football too. I was going to have eaten raw meat, and dumb-belled, to make myself strong enough to thrash you," added Charles remorsefully.

"Eat a butcher's shop full, if you like," replied Philip with contempt. And I think it showed that Charles was beginning to practise forbearance, that he made no reply.

* * * * *

Some years have passed since those Twelfth Night theatricals. The Dragon has long been dissolved into his component scales, and we never have impromptu performances now. The passing fame which a terrible railway accident gave to our insignificant station has also faded. But it set a seal on our good resolutions which I may honestly say has not been lightly broken.

There, on the very spot where I had almost resolved never to forgive Philip, never to try to heal the miserable wounds of the family peace, I learned the news of the accident in which he might have been killed. Philip says that if anything could make him behave better to me it is the thought that I saved his life, as he calls it. But if anything could help me to be good to him, surely it must be the remembrance of how nearly I did not save him.

I put Alice on an equality in our bedroom that night, and gave her part-ownership of the text and the picture. We are very happy together.

We have all tried to improve, and I think I may say we have been fairly successful.

More than once I have heard (one does hear many things people say behind one's back) that new acquaintances— people who have only known us lately—have expressed astonishment, not unmixed with a generous indignation, on hearing that we were ever described by our friends as—A VERY ILL-TEMPERED FAMILY.

OUR FIELD

Though nothing can bring back the hour
Of splendour in the grass, of glory in the flower;
We will grieve not, rather find
Strength in what remains behind,
In the primal sympathy
Which, having been, must ever be.

* * * * *

And, O ye fountains, meadows, hills, and groves,
Think not of any severing of our loves!
Yet in my heart of hearts I feel your might;

* * * * *

Thanks to the human heart by which we live,
Thanks to its tenderness, its joys, and fears:
To me the meanest flower that blows can give
Thoughts that do often lie too deep for tears.

—Wordsworth

OUR FIELD

There were four of us, and three of us had godfathers and godmothers. Three each. Three times three make nine, and not a fairy godmother in the lot. That was what vexed us.

It was very provoking, because we knew so well what we wanted if we had one, and she had given us three wishes each. Three times three make nine. We could have got all we wanted out of nine wishes, and have provided for Perronet into the bargain. It would not have been any good Perronet having wishes all to himself, because he was only a dog.

We never knew who it was that drowned Perronet, but it was Sandy who saved his life and brought him home. It was when he was coming home from school, and he brought Perronet with him. Perronet was not at all nice to look at when we first saw him, though we were very sorry for him. He was wet all over, and his eyes shut, and you could see his ribs, and he looked quite dark and sticky. But when he dried, he dried a lovely yellow, with two black ears like velvet. People sometimes asked us what kind of dog he was, but we never knew, except that he was the nicest possible kind.

When we had got him, we were afraid we were not going to be allowed to have him. Mother said we could not afford him, because of the tax and his keep. The tax was five shillings, but there wanted nearly a year to the time of paying it. Of course his keep began as soon as he could eat, and that was the very same evening. We were all very miserable, because we were so fond of Perronet—at least, Perronet was not his name then, but he was the same person—and at last it was settled that all three of us would give up sugar, towards saving the expense of his keep, if he might stay. It was hardest for Sandy, because he was particularly fond of sweet

Juliana Horatia Ewing

things; but then he was particularly fond of Perronet. So we all gave up sugar, and Perronet was allowed to remain.

About the tax, we thought we could save any pennies or half-pennies we got during the year, and it was such a long time to the time for paying, that we should be almost sure to have enough by then. We had not any money at the time, or we should have bought a savings-box; but lots of people save their money in stockings, and we settled that we would. An old stocking would not do, because of the holes, and I had not many good pairs; but we took one of my winter ones to use in the summer, and then we thought we could pour the money into one of my good summer ones when the winter came.

What we most of all wanted a fairy godmother for was about our "homes." There was no kind of play we liked better than playing at houses and new homes. But no matter where we made our "home," it was sure to be disturbed. If it was indoors, and we made a palace under the big table, as soon as ever we had got it nicely divided into rooms according to where the legs came, it was certain to be dinner-time, and people put their feet into it. The nicest house we ever had was in the out-house; we had it, and kept it quite a secret, for weeks. And then the new load of wood came and covered up everything, our best oyster-shell dinner-service and all.

Any one can see that it is impossible really to fancy anything when you are constantly interrupted. You can't have any fun out of a railway train stopping at stations, when they take all your carriages to pieces because the chairs are wanted for tea; any more than you can play properly at Grace Darling in a life-boat, when they say the old cradle is too good to be knocked about in that way.

It was always the same. If we wanted to play at Thames

Tunnel under the beds, we were not allowed; and the day we did Aladdin in the store-closet, old Jane came and would put away the soap, just when Aladdin could not possibly have got the door of the cave open.

It was one day early in May—a very hot day for the time of year, which had made us rather cross—when Sandy came in about four o'clock, smiling more broadly even than usual, and said to Richard and me, "I've got a fairy godmother, and she's given us a field."

Sandy was very fond of eating, especially sweet things. He used to keep back things from meals to enjoy afterwards, and he almost always had a piece of cake in his pocket. He brought a piece out now, and took a large mouthful, laughing at us with his eyes over the top of it.

"What's the good of a field?" said Richard.

"Splendid houses in it," said Sandy.

"I'm quite tired of fancying homes," said I. "It's no good; we always get turned out."

"It's quite a new place," Sandy continued; "you've never been there," and he took a triumphant bite of the cake.

"How did you get there?" asked Richard.

"The fairy godmother showed me," was Sandy's reply.

There is such a thing as nursery honour. We respected each other's pretendings unless we were very cross, but I didn't disbelieve in his fairy godmother. I only said, "You shouldn't talk with your mouth full," to snub him for making a secret about his field.

Sandy is very good-tempered. He only laughed and said, "Come along. It's much cooler out now. The sun's going down."

He took us along Gipsy Lane. We had been there once or twice, for walks, but not very often, for there was some horrid story about it which rather frightened us. I do not know what it was, but it was a horrid one. Still we had been there, and I knew it quite well. At the end of it there is a stile, by which you go into a field, and at the other end you get over another stile, and find yourself in the high road.

"If this is our field, Sandy," said I, when we got to the first stile, "I'm very sorry, but it really won't do. I know that lots of people come through it. We should never be quiet here."

Sandy laughed. He didn't speak, and he didn't get over the stile; he went through a gate close by it leading into a little sort of bye-lane that was all mud in winter and hard cart-ruts in summer. I had never been up it, but I had seen hay and that sort of thing go in and come out of it.

He went on and we followed him. The ruts were very disagreeable to walk on, but presently he led us through a hole in the hedge, and we got into a field. It was a very bare-looking field, and went rather uphill. There was no path, but Sandy walked away up it, and we went after him. There was another hedge at the top, and a stile in it. It had very rough posts, one much longer than the other, and the cross step was gone, but there were two rails, and we all climbed over. And when we got to the other side, Sandy leaned against the big post and gave a wave with his right hand and said, "This is our field."

It sloped down hill, and the hedges round it were rather high, with awkward branches of blackthorn sticking out here and there without any leaves, and with the blossom lying white on the black twigs like snow. There were cowslips all over the field, but they were thicker at the lower end, which was damp. The great heat of the day was over. The sun shone still, but it shone low down and made such splendid shadows that we all walked about with grey giants at our feet; and it made the bright green of the grass, and the cowslips down below, and the top of the hedge, and Sandy's hair, and everything in the sun and the mist behind the elder bush which was out of the sun, so yellow—so very yellow—that just for a minute I really believed about Sandy's godmother, and thought it was a story come true, and that everything was turning into gold.

But it was only for a minute; of course I know that fairy tales are not true. But it was a lovely field, and when we had put our hands to our eyes and had a good look at it, I said to Sandy, "I beg your pardon, Sandy, for telling you not to talk with your mouth full. It is the best field I ever heard of."

"Sit down," said Sandy, doing the honours; and we all sat down under the hedge.

"There are violets just behind us," he continued. "Can't you smell them? But whatever you do, don't tell anybody of those, or we shan't keep our field to ourselves for a day. And look here." He had turned over on to his face, and Richard and I did the same, whilst Sandy fumbled among the bleached grass and brown leaves.

"Hyacinths," said Richard, as Sandy displayed the green tops of them.

"As thick as peas," said Sandy. "This bank will be blue in a few weeks; and fiddle-heads everywhere. There will be no end of ferns. May to any extent—it's only in bud yet—and there's a wren's nest in there—" At this point he rolled suddenly over on to his back and looked up.

"A lark," he explained; "there was one singing its head off, this morning. I say, Dick, this will be a good field for a kite, won't it? *But wait a bit.*"

After every fresh thing that Sandy showed us in our field, he always finished by saying, "*Wait a bit*"; and that was because there was always something else better still.

"There's a brook at the bottom there," he said, "with lots of fresh-water shrimps. I wonder whether they would boil red. *But wait a bit.* This hedge, you see, has got a very high bank, and it's worn into kind of ledges. I think we could play at 'shops' there—*but wait a bit.*"

"It's almost *too* good, Sandy dear!" said I, as we crossed the field to the opposite hedge.

"The best is to come," said Sandy. "I've a very good mind not to let it out till to-morrow." And to our distraction he sat down in the middle of the field, put his arms round his knees, as if we were playing at "Honey-pots," and rocked himself backwards and forwards with a face of brimming satisfaction.

Neither Richard nor I would have been so mean as to explore on our own account, when the field was Sandy's discovery, but we tried hard to persuade him to show us everything.

He had the most provoking way of laughing and holding his tongue, and he did that now, besides slowly turning all his pockets inside-out into his hands, and mumbling up the crumbs and odd currants, saying, "Guess!" between every mouthful.

But when there was not a crumb left in the seams of his pockets, Sandy turned them back, and jumping up, said— "One can only tell a secret once. It's a hollow oak. Come along!"

He ran and we ran, to the other side of Our Field. I had read of hollow oaks, and seen pictures of them, and once I dreamed of one, with a witch inside, but we had never had one to play in. We were nearly wild with delight. It looked all solid from the field, but when we pushed behind, on the hedge side, there was the door, and I crept in, and it smelt of wood, and delicious damp. There could not be a more perfect castle, and though there were no windows in the sides, the light came in from the top, where the polypody hung over like a fringe. Sandy was quite right. It was the very best thing in Our Field.

Perronet was as fond of the field as we were. What he liked were the little birds. At least, I don't know that he liked them, but they were what he chiefly attended to. I think he knew that it was our field, and thought he was the watch-dog of it, and whenever a bird settled down anywhere, he barked at it, and then it flew away, and he ran barking after it till he lost it; and by that time another had settled down, and then Perronet flew at him, and so on, all up and down the hedge. He never caught a bird, and never would let one sit down, if he could see it.

We had all kinds of games in Our Field. Shops—for there were quantities of things to sell—and sometimes I was a moss-merchant, for there were ten different kinds of moss by the brook, and sometimes I was a jeweller, and sold daisy-chains and pebbles, and coral sets made of holly berries, and oak-apple necklaces; and sometimes I kept provisions, like earth-nuts and mallow-cheeses, and mushrooms; and some-times I kept a flower-shop, and sold nosegays and wreaths, and umbrellas made of rushes, I liked that kind of shop, because I am fond of arranging flowers, and I always make our birthday wreaths. And sometimes I kept a whole lot of shops, and Richard and Sandy bought my things, and paid for them with money made of elder-pith, sliced into rounds. The first shop I kept was to sell cowslips, and Richard and Sandy lived by the brook, and were wine merchants, and made cowslip wine in a tin mug.

The elder-tree was a beauty. In July the cream-coloured flowers were so sweet, we could hardly sit under it, and in the autumn it was covered with berries; but we were always a little disappointed that they never tasted in the least like elderberry syrup. Richard used to make flutes out of the stalks, and one really did to play tunes on, but it always made Perronet bark.

Richard's every-day cap had a large hole in the top, and when we were in Our Field we always hung it on the top of the tallest of the two stile-posts, to show that we were there; just as the Queen has a flag hung out at Windsor Castle, when she is at home.

We played at castles and houses, and when we were tired of the houses, we pretended to pack up, and went to the seaside for change of air by the brook. Sandy and I took off our shoes and stockings and were bathing-women, and we bathed Perronet; and Richard sat on the bank and was a "tripper," looking at us through a telescope; for when the elder-stems cracked and wouldn't do for flutes, he made them into telescopes. And before we went down to the brook we made jam of hips and haws from the hedge at the top of the field, and put it into acorn cups, and took it with us, that the children might not be short of rolypolies at the seaside.

Whatever we played at we were never disturbed. Birds, and

cows, and men and horses ploughing in the distance, do not disturb you at all.

We were very happy that summer: the boys were quite happy, and the only thing that vexed me was thinking of Perronet's tax-money. For months and months went on and we did not save it. Once we got as far as twopence half-penny, and then one day Richard came to me and said, "I must have some more string for the kite. You might lend me a penny out of Perronet's stocking, till I get some money of my own."

So I did; and the next day Sandy came and said, "You lent Dick one of Perronet's coppers; I'm sure Perronet would lend me one," and then they said it was ridiculous to leave a half-penny there by itself, so we spent it in acid drops.

It worried me so much at last, that I began to dream horrible dreams about Perronet having to go away because we hadn't saved his tax-money. And then I used to wake up and cry, till the pillow was so wet, I had to turn it. The boys never seemed to mind, but then boys don't think about things; so that I was quite surprised when one day I found Sandy alone in our field with Perronet in his arms, crying, and feeding him with cake; and I found he was crying about the tax-money.

I cannot bear to see boys cry. I would much rather cry myself, and I begged Sandy to leave off, for I said I was quite determined to try and think of something.

It certainly was remarkable that the very next day should be the day when we heard about the flower-show.

It was in school—the village school, for Mother could not afford to send us anywhere else—and the schoolmaster rapped on his desk and said, "Silence, children!" and that at the agricultural show there was to be a flower-show this year, and that an old gentleman was going to give prizes to the school-children for window-plants and for the best arranged wild flowers. There were to be nosegays and wreaths, and there was to be a first prize of five shillings, and a second prize of half-a-crown, for the best collection of wild flowers with the names put to them.

"The English names," said the schoolmaster; "and there may be—silence, children!—there may be collections of ferns, or grasses, or mosses to compete, too, for the gentleman wishes to encourage a taste for natural history."

And several of the village children said, "What's that?" and I squeezed Sandy's arm, who was sitting next to me, and whispered, "Five shillings!" and the schoolmaster said, "Silence, children!" and I thought I never should have finished my lessons that day for thinking of Perronet's tax-money.

July is not at all a good month for wild flowers; May and June are far better. However, the show was to be in the first week in July.

I said to the boys, "Look here: I'll do a collection of flowers. I know the names, and I can print. It's no good two or three people muddling with arranging flowers; but; if you will get me what I want, I shall be very much obliged. If either of you will make another collection, you know there are ten kinds of mosses by the brook; and we have names for them of our own, and they are English. Perhaps they'll do. But everything must come out of Our Field."

The boys agreed, and they were very good. Richard made me a box, rather high at the back. We put sand at the bottom and damped it, and then Feather Moss, lovely clumps of it, and into that I stuck the flowers. They all came out of Our Field. I like to see grass with flowers, and we had very pretty grasses, and between every bunch of flowers I put a bunch of grass of different kinds. I got all the flowers and all the grasses ready first, and printed the names on pieces of cardboard to stick in with them, and then I arranged them by my eye, and Sandy handed me what I called for, for Richard was busy at the brook making a tray of mosses.

Sandy knew the flowers and the names of them quite as well as I did, of course; we knew everything that lived in Our Field; so when I called, "Ox-eye daisies, cock's-foot grass, labels; meadow-sweet, fox-tail grass, labels; dog-roses, shivering grass, labels;" and so on, he gave me the right things, and I had nothing to do but to put the colours that looked best together next to each other, and to make the grass look light, and pull up bits of moss to show well. And at the very end I put in a label, "All out of Our Field."

I did not like it when it was done; but Richard praised it so much, it cheered me up, and I thought his mosses looked lovely.

The flower-show day was very hot. I did not think it could be hotter anywhere in the world than it was in the field where the show was; but it was hotter in the tent.

We should never have got in at all—for you had to pay at the gate—but they let competitors in free, though not at first. When we got in, there were a lot of grown-up people, and it was very hard work getting along among them, and getting to see the stands with the things on. We kept seeing tickets with "1st Prize" and "2nd Prize," and struggling up; but they were sure to be dahlias in a tray, or fruit that you mightn't eat, or vegetables. The vegetables disappointed us so often, I got to hate them. I don't think I shall ever like very big potatoes (before they are boiled) again, particularly the red ones. It makes me feel sick with heat and anxiety to think of them.

We had struggled slowly all round the tent, and seen all the cucumbers, onions, lettuces, long potatoes, round potatoes, and everything else, when we saw an old gentleman, with spectacles and white hair, standing with two or three ladies. And then we saw three nosegays in jugs, with all the green picked off, and the flowers tied as tightly together as they would go, and then we saw some prettier ones, and then we saw my collection, and it had got a big label in it marked "1st Prize," and next to it came Richard's moss-tray, with the Hair-moss, and the Pincushion-moss, and the Scale-mosses, and a lot of others with names of our own, and it was marked "2nd Prize." And I gripped one of Sandy's arms just as Richard seized the other, and we both cried, "Perronet is paid for!"

* * * * *

There was two-and-sixpence over. We never had such a feast! It was a picnic tea, and we had it in Our Field. I thought Sandy and Perronet would have died of cake, but they were none the worse.

We were very much frightened at first when the old gentleman invited himself; but he would come, and he brought a lot of nuts, and he did get inside the oak, though it is really too small for him.

I don't think there ever was anybody so kind. If he were not a man, I should really and truly believe in Sandy's fairy godmother.

Of course I don't really believe in fairies. I am not so young as that. And I know that Our Field does not exactly belong to us.

I wonder to whom it does belong? Richard says he believes it belongs to the gentleman who lives at the big red house among the trees. But he must be wrong; for we see that gentleman at church every Sunday, but we never saw him in Our Field.

And I don't believe anybody could have such a field of their very own, and never come to see it, from one end of Summer to the other.

Juliana Horatia Ewing

MADAM LIBERALITY

"Like little body with a mighty heart."

—*King Henry V., Act 2*

PART I

It was not her real name: it was given to her by her brothers and sister. People with very marked qualities of character do sometimes get such distinctive titles, to rectify the indefiniteness of those they inherit and those they receive in baptism. The ruling peculiarity of a character is apt to show itself early in life, and it showed itself in Madam Liberality when she was a little child.

Plum-cakes were not plentiful in her home when Madam Liberality was young, and such as there were, were of the "wholesome" kind—plenty of bread-stuff, and the currants and raisins at a respectful distance from each other. But few as the plums were, she seldom ate them. She picked them out very carefully, and put them into a box, which was hidden under her pinafore.

When we grown-up people were children, and plum-cake and plum-pudding tasted very much nicer than they do now, we also picked out the plums. Some of us ate them at once, and had then to toil slowly through the cake or pudding, and some valiantly dispatched the plainer portion of the feast at the beginning, and kept the plums to sweeten the end. Sooner or later we ate them ourselves, but Madam Liberality kept her plums for other people.

When the vulgar meal was over—that commonplace refreshment ordained and superintended by the elders of the household—Madam Liberality would withdraw into a corner, from which she issued notes of invitation to all the dolls. They were "fancy written" on curl papers and folded into cocked hats.

Then began the real feast. The dolls came, and the children with them. Madam Liberality had no toy tea-sets or dinner-sets, but there were acorn-cups filled to the brim, and the water tasted deliciously, though it came out of the ewer in the night nursery, and had not even been filtered. And before every doll was a flat oyster-shell covered with a round oyster-shell, a complete set of complete pairs, which had been collected by degrees, like old family plate. And when the upper shell was raised, on every dish lay a plum. It was then that Madam Liberality got her sweetness out of the cake.

She was in her glory at the head of the inverted tea-chest; and if the raisins would not go round, the empty oyster-shell was hers, and nothing offended her more than to have this noticed. That was her spirit, then and always. She could "do without" anything, if the wherewithal to be hospitable was left to her.

When one's brain is no stronger than mine is, one gets very

Juliana Horatia Ewing

much confused in disentangling motives and nice points of character. I have doubted whether Madam Liberality's besetting virtue were a virtue at all. Was it unselfishness or a love of approbation, benevolence or fussiness, the gift of sympathy or the lust of power? Or was it something else? She was a very sickly child, with much pain to bear, and many pleasures to forego. Was it, as doctors say, "an effort of nature," to make her live outside herself and be happy in the happiness of others?

Equal doubt may hang over the conduct of her brothers and sister towards her. Did they more love her, or find her useful? Was their gratitude—as gratitude has been defined to be—"a keen sense of favours to come"? They certainly got used to her services, and to begging and borrowing the few things that were her "very own," without fear of refusal. But if they rather took her benevolence for granted, and thought that she "liked lending her things," and that it was her way of enjoying possessions, they may have been right; for next to one's own soul, one's own family is perhaps the best judge of one's temper and disposition.

And they called her Madam Liberality, so Madam Liberality she shall remain.

It has been hinted that there was a reason for the scarceness of the plums in the plum-cake. Madam Liberality's father was dead, and her mother was very poor, and had several children. It was not an easy matter with her to find bread for the family, putting currants and raisins out of the question.

Though poor, they were, however, gentle-folk, and had, for that matter, rich relations. Very rich relations indeed! Madam Liberality's mother's first cousin had fifteen thousand a year. His servants did not spend ten thousand. (As to what he spent himself, it was comparatively trifling.) The rest of the money accumulated. Not that it was being got together to do something with by and by. He had no intention of ever spending more than he spent at present. Indeed, with a lump of coal taken off here, and a needless candle blown out there, he rather hoped in future to spend less.

His wife was Madam Liberality's godmother. She was a good-hearted woman, and took real pleasure in being kind to people, in the way she thought best for them. Sometimes it was a graceful and appropriate way, and very often it was not. The most acceptable act of kindness she ever did to her god-daughter was when the child was recovering from an illness, and she asked her to visit her at the seaside.

Madam Liberality had never seen the sea, and the thought of it proved a better stimulus than the port wine which her doctor ordered so easily, and her mother got with such difficulty.

When new clothes were bought, or old ones refurbished, Madam Liberality, as a rule, went to the wall. Not because her mother was ever guilty of favouritism, but because such occasions afforded an opportunity of displaying generosity towards her younger sister.

But this time it was otherwise; for whatever could be spared towards "summer things" for the two little girls was spent upon Madam Liberality's outfit for the seaside. There was a new dress, and a jacket "as good as new," for it was cut out of "mother's" cloth cloak and made up, with the best binding and buttons in the shop, by the village tailor. And he was bribed, in a secret visit, and with much coaxing from the little girls, to make real pockets instead of braided shams. The *second best* frock was compounded of two which had hitherto been *very bests*—Madam Liberality's own, eked out by "Darling's" into a more fashionable fullness, and with a cape to match.

There was a sense of solid property to be derived from being able to take in at a glance the stock of well-mended undergarments, half of which were generally at the wash. Besides, they had been added to, and all the stockings were darned, and only one pair in the legs where it would show, below short petticoat mark.

Then there was a bonnet newly turned and trimmed, and a pair and a half of new boots, for surely boots are at least half new when they have been (as the village cobbler described it in his bill) "souled and healed"?

Poor little Madam Liberality! When she saw the things which covered her bed in their abundance, it seemed to her an outfit for a princess. And yet when her godmother asked Podmore, the lady's-maid, "How is the child off for clothes?" Podmore unhesitatingly replied, "She've nothing fit to be seen, ma'am," which shows how differently the same things appear in different circumstances.

Podmore was a good friend to Madam Liberality. She had that open-handed spirit which one acquires quite naturally in a house where everything goes on on a large scale, at somebody else's expense. Now Madam Liberality's godmother, from the very largeness of her possessions, was obliged to leave the care of them to others, in such matters as food, dress, the gardens, the stables, etc. So, like many other people in a similar case, she amused herself and exercised her economical instincts by troublesome little thriftinesses, by making cheap presents, dear bargains, and so forth. She was by nature a managing woman; and when those very grand people, the butler, the housekeeper, the head-gardener, and the lady's-maid had divided her household duties among them, there was nothing left for her to be clever about, except such little matters as joining the fag-ends of the bronze sealing-wax sticks which lay in the silver inkstand on the malachite writing-table, and being good-natured at the cheapest rate at which her friends could be benefited.

Madam Liberality's best neckerchief had been very pretty when it was new, and would have been pretty as well as clean still if the washerwoman had not used rather too hot an iron to it, so that the blue in the check pattern was somewhat faded. And yet it had felt very smart as Madam Liberality drove in the carrier's cart to meet the coach at the outset of her journey. But when she sat against the rich blue leather of her godmother's coach as they drove up and down the esplanade, it was like looking at fairy jewels by daylight when they turn into faded leaves.

"Is that your best neckerchief, child?" said the old lady.

"Yes, ma'am," blushed Madam Liberality,

So when they got home her godmother went to her odds-and-ends drawer.

Podmore never interfered with this drawer. She was content to be despotic among the dresses, and left the old lady to faddle to her heart's content with bits of old lace and ribbon which she herself would not have condescended to wear.

The old lady fumbled them over. There were a good many half-yards of ribbon with very large patterns, but nothing really fit for Madam Liberality's little neck but a small Indian scarf of many-coloured silk. It was old, and Podmore would never have allowed her mistress to drive on the esplanade in anything so small and youthful-looking; but the colours were quite bright, and there was no doubt but that Madam Liberality might be provided for by a cheaper neck-ribbon.

Juliana Horatia Ewing

So the old lady shut the drawer, and toddled down the corridor that led to Podmore's room.

She had a good general idea that Podmore's perquisites were large, but perquisites seem to be a condition of valuable servants in large establishments, and then anything which could be recovered from what had already passed into Podmore's room must be a kind of economy. So she resolved that Podmore should "find something" for Madam Liberality's neck.

"I never noticed it, ma'am, till I brought your shawl to the carriage," said Podmore. "If I had seen it before, the young lady shouldn't have come with you so. I'll see to it, ma'am."

"Thank you, Podmore."

"Can you spare me to go into the town this afternoon, ma'am?" added the lady's-maid. "I want some things at Huckaback and Woolsey's."

Huckaback and Woolsey were the linendrapers where Madam Liberality's godmother "had an account." It was one of the things on a large scale over the details of which she had no control.

"You'll be back in time to dress me?"

"Oh dear, yes, ma'am." And having settled the old lady's shawl on her shoulders, and drawn out her cap-lappets, Podmore returned to her work.

It was a work of kindness. The old lady might deal shabbily with her faded ribbons and her relations, but the butler, the housekeeper, and the lady's-maid did their best to keep up the credit of the family.

It was well known that Madam Liberality was a cousin, and Podmore resolved that she should have a proper frock to go down to dessert in.

So she had been very busy making a little slip out of a few yards of blue silk which had been over and above one of the old lady's dresses, and now she betook herself to the draper's to get spotted muslin to cover it and ribbons to trim it with.

And whilst Madam Liberality's godmother was still feeling a few twinges about the Indian scarf, Podmore ordered a pink neckerchief shot with white, and with pink and white fringes, to be included in the parcel.

But it was not in this way alone that Podmore was a good friend to Madam Liberality.

She took her out walking, and let her play on the beach, and even bring home dirty weeds and shells. Indeed, Podmore herself was not above collecting cowries in a pill-box for her little nephews.

When Mrs. Podmore met acquaintances on the beach, Madam Liberality played alone, and these were her happiest moments. She played amongst the rotting, weed-grown stakes of an old pier, and "fancied" rooms among them—suites of rooms in which she would lodge her brothers and sister if they came to visit her, and where—with cockle-shells for teacups, and lava for vegetables, and fucus-pods for fish—they should find themselves as much enchanted as Beauty in the palace of the Beast.

Again and again she "fancied" Darling into her shore-palace, the delights of which should only be marred by the growls which she herself would utter from time to time from behind the stakes, in the character of a sea-beast, and which should but enhance the moment when she would rush out and throw her arms round Darling's neck and reveal herself as Madam Liberality.

"Darling" was the pet name of Madam Liberality's sister— her only sister, on whom she lavished the intensest affection of a heart which was always a large one in proportion to her little body. It seemed so strange to play at any game of fancies without Darling, that Madam Liberality could hardly realize it.

She might be preparing by herself a larger treat than usual for the others; but it was incredible that no one would come after all, and that Darling would never see the palace on the beach, and the state-rooms, and the limpets, and the seaweed, and the salt-water soup, and the real fish (a small dab discarded from a herring-net) which Madam Liberality had got for her.

Her mind was filled with day-dreams of Darling's coming, and of how she would display to her all the wonders of the seashore, which would reflect almost as much credit upon her as if she had invented razor-shells and crabs. She thought so much about it that she began quite to expect it.

Was it not natural that her godmother should see that she must be lonely, and ask Darling to come and be with her? Perhaps the old lady had already done so, and the visit was to be a surprise. Madam Liberality could quite imagine doing a nice thing like this herself, and she hoped it so strongly that she almost came to believe in it.

Every day she waited hopefully, first for the post, and then for the time when the coach came in, the hour at which she herself had arrived; but the coach brought no Darling, and the post brought no letter to say that she was coming, and

Madam Liberality's hopes were disappointed.

Madam Liberality was accustomed to disappointment.

From her earliest years it had been a family joke that poor Madam Liberality was always in ill-luck's way.

It is true that she was constantly planning; and if one builds castles, one must expect a few loose stones about one's ears now and then. But, besides this, her little hopes were constantly being frustrated by fate.

If the pigs or the hens got into the garden, Madam Liberality's bed was sure to be laid waste before any one came to the rescue. When a picnic or a tea-party was in store, if Madam Liberality did not catch cold, so as to hinder her from going, she was pretty sure to have a quinsy from fatigue or wet feet afterwards. When she had a treat she paid for the pleasurable excitement by a headache, just as when she ate sweet things they gave her toothache.

But if her luck was less than other people's, her courage and good spirits were more than common. She could think with pleasure about the treat when she had forgotten the headache. One side of her little face would look fairly cheerful when the other was obliterated by a flannel bag of hot camomile flowers, and the whole was redolent of every horrible domestic remedy for toothache, from oil of cloves and creosote to a baked onion in the ear. No sufferings abated her energy for fresh exploits, or quenched the hope that cold, and damp, and fatigue would not hurt her "this time."

In the intervals of wringing out hot flannels for her own quinsy, she would amuse herself by devising a desert island expedition on a larger and possibly a damper scale than hitherto, against the time when she should be out again.

It is a very old simile, but Madam Liberality really was like a cork rising on the top of the very wave of ill-luck that had swallowed up her hopes. Her little white face and undaunted spirit bobbed up after each mischance or malady as ready and hopeful as ever.

Though her day-dream about Darling and the shore palace was constantly disappointed, this did not hinder her from indulging new hopes and fancies in another place to which she went with Podmore; a place which was filled with wonders of a different kind from the treasures of the palace on the shore.

It was called the Bazaar. It would be a very long business to say what was in it. But amongst other things there were foreign cage-birds, musical-boxes, and camp-stools, and baskets, and polished pebbles, and paper patterns, and a little ladies' and children's millinery, and a good deal of mock jewellery, and some very bad soaps and scents, and some very good children's toys.

It was Madam Liberality's godmother who first took her to the bazaar. A titled lady of her acquaintance had heard that wire flower-baskets of a certain shape could be bought in the bazaar cheaper (by two-pence-halfpenny each) than in London; and after writing to her friend to ascertain the truth of the statement, she wrote again to authorize her to purchase three on her behalf. So Madam Liberality's godmother ordered out the blue carriage and pair, and drove with her little cousin to the bazaar.

And as they came out, followed by a bearded man, bowing very low, and carrying the wire baskets, Madam Liberality's godmother stopped near the toy-stall to button her glove. And when she had buttoned it (which took a long time, because her hands were stout, and Podmore generally did it with a hook), she said to Madam Liberality, "Now, child, I want to tell you that if you are very good whilst you are with me, and Podmore gives me a good report of you, I will bring you here before you go home, and buy you a present."

Madam Liberality's heart danced with delight. She wished her godmother would stand by the toy-stall for an hour, that she might see what she most hoped the present would be. But the footman tucked them into the carriage, and the bearded man bowed himself back into the bazaar, and they drove home. Then Madam Liberality's godmother directed the butler to dispatch the wire baskets to her ladyship, which he did by coach. And her ladyship's butler paid the carriage, and tipped the man who brought the parcel from the coach-office, and charged these items in his account. And her ladyship wrote a long letter of thanks to Madam Liberality's godmother for her kindness in saving her unnecessary expense.

The old lady did not go to the bazaar again for some time, but Madam Liberality went there with Podmore. She looked at the toys and wondered which of them might one day be her very own. The white china tea-service with the green rim, big enough to make real tea in, was too good to be hoped for, but there were tin tea-sets where the lids would come off, and wooden ones where they were stuck on; and there were all manner of toys that would be invaluable for all kinds of nursery games and fancies.

They helped a "fancy" of Madam Liberality even then. She used to stand by the toy-stall, and fancy that she was as rich as her godmother, and was going to give Christmas-boxes to her brothers and sister, and her amusement was to choose, though she could not buy them.

Out of this came a deep mortification. She had been playing

at this fancy one afternoon, and having rather confused herself by changing her mind about the toys, she went through her final list in an undertone, to get it clearly into her head. The shopman was serving a lady, and Madam Liberality thought he could not hear her as she murmured, "The china tea-set, the box of beasts, the doll's furniture for Darling," etc., etc. But the shopman's hearing was very acute, and he darted forward, crying, "The china tea-set, did you say, miss?"

The blood rushed up to poor Madam Liberality's face till it seemed to choke her, and the lady, whom the shopman had been serving, said kindly, "I think the little girl said the box of beasts."

Madam Liberality hoped it was a dream, but having pinched herself, she found that it was not.

Her mother had often said to her, "When you can't think what to say, tell the truth." It was not a very easy rule, but Madam Liberality went by it.

"I don't want anything, thank you," said she; "at least, I mean I have no money to buy anything with: I was only counting the things I should like to get if I had."

And then, as the floor of the bazaar would *not* open and swallow her up, she ran away, with her red face and her empty pocket, to shelter herself with Podmore at the mock-jewellery stall, and she did not go to the bazaar any more.

Once again disappointment was in store for Madam Liberality. The end of her visit came, and her godmother's promise seemed to be forgotten. But the-night before her departure, the old lady came into her room and said,

"I couldn't take you with me to-day, child, but I didn't forget my promise. Podmore says you've been very good, and so I've brought you a present. A very *useful* one, I hope," added the old lady, in a tone as if she were congratulating herself upon her good sense. "And tell Catherine—that's your mother, child—with my love, always to have you dressed for the evening. I like to see children come in to dessert, when they have good manners—which I must say you have; besides, it keeps the nurses up to their work."

And then she drew out from its paper a little frock of pink *mousseline-de-laine*, very prettily tacked together by the young woman at the millinery-stall, and very cheap for its gay appearance.

Down came all Madam Liberality's visions in connection with the toy-stall: but she consoled herself that night with picturing Darling's delight when she gave her (as she meant to give her) the pink dress.

She had another source of comfort and anticipation—*the scallop-shells*.

But this requires to be explained. The greatest prize which Madam Liberality had gained from her wanderings by the seashore was a complete scallop-shell. When washed the double shell was as clean and as pretty as any china muffin-dish with a round top; and now her ambition was to get four more, and thus to have a service for doll's feasts which should far surpass the oyster-shells. She was talking about this to Podmore one day when they were picking cowries together, and Podmore cried, "Why, this little girl would get you them, miss, I'll be bound!"

She was a bare-footed little girl, who sold pebbles and seaweed, and salt water for sponging with, and she had undertaken to get the scallop-shells, and had run off to pick seaweed out of a newly landed net before Madam Liberality could say "Thank you."

She heard no more of the shells, however, until the day before she went away, when the butler met her as she came indoors, and told her that the little girl was waiting. And it was not till Madam Liberality saw the scallop-shells lying clean and pink in a cotton handkerchief that she remembered that she had no money to pay for them.

Here was another occasion for painful truthtelling! But to make humiliating confession before the butler seemed almost beyond even Madam Liberality's moral courage. He went back to his pantry, however, and she pulled off her pretty pink neckerchief and said,

"I am *very* sorry, little girl, but I've got no money of my own; but if you would like this instead—" And the little girl seemed quite pleased with her bargain, and ran hastily off, as if afraid that the young lady would change her mind.

And this was how Madam Liberality got her scallop-shells.

* * * * *

It may seem strange that Madam Liberality should ever have been accused of meanness, and yet her eldest brother did once shake his head at her and say, "You're the most meanest and the *generoustest* person I ever knew!" And Madam Liberality wept over the accusation, although her brother was then too young to form either his words or his opinions correctly.

But it was the touch of truth in it which made Madam Liberality cry. To the end of their lives Tom and she were alike and yet different in this matter. Madam Liberality saved, and pinched, and planned, and then gave away, and Tom gave away without the pinching and saving. This sounds much handsomer, and it was poor Tom's misfortune that he always believed it to be so; though he gave away what did not belong to him, and fell back for the supply of his own pretty numerous wants upon other people, not forgetting Madam Liberality.

Painful experience convinced Madam Liberality in the end that his way was a wrong one, but she had her doubts many times in her life whether there were not something unhandsome in her own decided talent for economy. Not that economy was always pleasant to her. When people are very poor for their position in life, they can only keep out of debt by stinting on many occasions when stinting is very painful to a liberal spirit. And it requires a sterner virtue than good-nature to hold fast the truth that it is nobler to be shabby and honest than to do things handsomely in debt.

But long before Tom had a bill even for bull's-eyes and Gibraltar Rock, Madam Liberality was pinching and plotting, and saving bits of coloured paper and ends of ribbon, with a thriftiness which seemed to justify Tom's view of her character.

The object of these savings was twofold: birthday presents and Christmas-boxes. They were the chief cares and triumphs of Madam Liberality's childhood. It was with the next birthday or the approaching Christmas in view that she saved her pence instead of spending them, but she so seldom had any money that she chiefly relied on her own ingenuity. Year by year it became more difficult to make anything which would "do for a boy;" but it was easy to please Darling, and "Mother's" unabated appreciation of pincushions, and of needle-books made out of old cards, was most satisfactory.

To break the mystery in which it always pleased Madam Liberality to shroud her small preparations, was to give her dire offence. As a rule, the others respected this caprice, and would even feign a little more surprise than they felt, upon occasion. But if during her preparations she had given umbrage to one of the boys, her retreat was soon invaded with cries of—"Ah! I see you, making birthday presents out of nothing and a quarter of a yard of ribbon!" Or—"There you are! At it again, with two old visiting cards and a ha'porth of flannel!" And only Darling's tenderest kisses could appease Madam Liberality's wrath and dry her tears.

She had never made a grander project for Christmas, or had greater difficulty in carrying it out, than in the winter which followed her visit to the seaside. It was in the house of her cousin that she had first heard of Christmas-trees, and to surprise the others with a Christmas-tree she was quite resolved. But as the time drew near, poor Madam Liberality was almost in despair about her presents, and this was doubly provoking, because a nice little fir-tree had been promised her. There was no blinking the fact that "Mother" had been provided with pincushions to repletion. And most of these made the needles rusty, from being stuffed with damp pig-meal, when the pigs and the pincushions were both being fattened for Christmas.

Madam Liberality sat with her little pale face on her hand and her slate before her, making her calculations. She wondered what emery-powder cost. Supposing it to be very cheap, and that she could get a quarter of a pound for "next to nothing," how useful a present might be made for "Mother" in the shape of an emery pincushion, to counteract the evil effects of the pig-meal ones! It would be a novelty even to Darling, especially if hers were made by glueing a tiny bag of emery into the mouth of a "boiled fowl cowry." Madam Liberality had seen such a pincushion in Podmore's work-basket. She had a shell of the kind, and the village carpenter would always let her put a stick into his glue-pot if she went to the shop.

But then, if emery were only a penny a pound, Madam Liberality had not a farthing to buy a quarter of a pound with. As she thought of this her brow contracted, partly with vexation, and partly because of a jumping pain in a big tooth, which, either from much illness or many medicines, or both, was now but the wreck of what a tooth should be. But as the toothache grew worse, a new hope dawned upon Madam Liberality. Perhaps one of her troubles would mend the other!

Being very tender-hearted over children's sufferings, it was her mother's custom to bribe rather than coerce when teeth had to be taken out. The fixed scale of reward was sixpence for a tooth without fangs, and a shilling for one with them. If pain were any evidence, this tooth certainly had fangs. But one does not have a tooth taken out if one can avoid it, and Madam Liberality bore bad nights and painful days till they could be endured no longer; and then, because she knew it distressed her mother to be present, she went alone to the doctor's house to ask him to take out her tooth.

The doctor was a very kind old man, and he did his best, so we will not say anything about his antique instruments, or the number of times he tied a pocket-handkerchief round an awful-looking claw, and put both into Madam Liberality's mouth without effect.

At last he said he had got the tooth out, and he wrapped it in paper, and gave it to Madam Liberality, who, having thought that it was her head he had extracted from its socket, was relieved to get away.

As she ran home she began to plan how to lay out her shilling for the best, and when she was nearly there she opened the bit of paper to look at her enemy, and it had no fangs!

"I'm *sure* it was more than a sixpenny one," she sobbed; "I believe he has left them in."

It involved more than the loss of half the funds she had reckoned upon. Perhaps this dreadful pain would go on even on Christmas Day. Her first thought was to carry her tears to her mother; her second that, if she only could be brave enough to have the fangs taken out, she might spare mother all distress about it till it was over, when she would certainly like her sufferings to be known and sympathized with. She knew well that courage does not come with waiting, and making a desperate rally of stout-heartedness, she ran back to the doctor.

He had gone out, but his assistant was in. He looked at Madam Liberality's mouth, and said that the fangs were certainly left in and would be much better out.

"Would it hurt *very* much?" asked Madam Liberality, trembling.

The assistant blinked the question of "hurting."

"I think I could do it," said he, "if you could sit still. Not if you were jumping about."

"I will sit still," said Madam Liberality.

"The boy shall hold your head," said the assistant.

But Madam Liberality rebelled; she could screw up her

sensitive nerves to endure the pain, but not to be coerced by "the boy."

"I give you my word of honour I will sit still," said she, with plaintive earnestness.

And the assistant (who had just remembered that the boy was out with the gig) said, "Very well, miss."

We need not dwell upon the next few seconds. The assistant kept his word, and Madam Liberality kept hers. She sat still, and went on sitting still after the operation was over till the assistant became alarmed, and revived her by pouring some choking stuff down her throat. After which she staggered to her feet and put out her hand and thanked him.

He was a strong, rough, good-natured young man, and little Madam Liberality's pale face and politeness touched him.

"You're the bravest little lady I ever knew," he said kindly; "and you keep your word like a queen. There's some stuff to put to the place, and there's sixpence, miss, if you'll take it, to buy lollipops with. You'll be able to eat them now."

After which he gave her an old pill-box to carry the fragments of her tooth in, and it was labelled "three to be taken at bed-time."

Madam Liberality staggered home, very giddy, but very happy. Moralists say a great deal about pain treading so very closely on the heels of pleasure in this life, but they are not always wise or grateful enough to speak of the pleasure which springs out of pain. And yet there is a bliss which comes just when pain has ceased, whose rapture rivals even the high happiness of unbroken health; and there is a keen relish about small pleasures hardly earned, in which the full measure of those who can afford anything they want is sometimes lacking.

Relief is certainly one of the most delicious sensations which poor humanity, can enjoy! Madam Liberality enjoyed it to the full, and she had more happiness yet in her cup, I fear praise was very pleasant to her, and the assistant had praised her, not undeservedly, and she knew that further praise was in store from the dearest source of approbation—from her mother. Ah! how pleased she would be! And so would Darling, who always cried when Madam Liberality was in great pain.

And this was only the beginning of pleasures. The sixpence would amply provide "goodies" for the Christmas-tree, and much might be done with the forthcoming shilling. And if her conduct on the present occasion would not support a request for a few ends of candles from the drawing-room candle-sticks, what profit would there be in being a heroine?

When her mother gave her two shillings instead of one, Madam Liberality felt in honour bound to say that she had already been rewarded with sixpence; but her mother only said,

"You quite deserved it, I'm sure," and she found herself in possession of no less than half-a-crown.

And now it is sad to relate that misfortune again overtook Madam Liberality. All the next day she longed to go into the village to buy sweetmeats, but it snowed and rained, and was bitterly cold, and she could not.

Just about dusk the weather slightly cleared up, and she picked her way through the melting snow to the shop. Her purchases were most satisfactory. How the boys would enjoy them! Madam Liberality enjoyed them already, though her face was still sore, and the pain had spread to her throat, and though her ideas seemed unusually brilliant, and her body pleasantly languid, which, added to a peculiar chill trembling of the knees—generally forewarned her of a coming quinsy. But warnings were thrown away upon Madam Liberality's obdurate hopefulness.

Just now she could think of nothing but the coming Christmas-tree. She hid the sweetmeats, and put her hand into her pocket for the two shillings, the exact outlay of which, in the neighbouring town, by means of the carrier, she had already arranged. But—the two shillings were gone! How she had lost them Madam Liberality had no idea.

She trudged through the dirty snow once more to the shop, and the counter was examined, and old Goody looked under the flour scales and in the big chinks of the stone floor. But the shillings were not there, and Madam Liberality kept her eyes on the pavement as she ran home, with as little result. Moreover, it was nearly dark.

It snowed heavily all night, and Madam Liberality slept very little from pain and anxiety; but this did not deter her from going out with the first daylight in the morning to rake among the snow near the door, although her throat was sore beyond concealment, her jaws stiff, and the pleasant languor and quick-wittedness had given way to restless fever.

Her conscience did prick her a little for the anxiety she was bringing upon her mother (her own sufferings she never forecast); but she could not give up her Christmas-tree without a struggle, and she hoped by a few familiar remedies to drive back the threatened illness.

Meanwhile, if the shillings were not found before eleven

o'clock it would be too late to send to the town shop by the carrier. But they were not found, and the old hooded cart rumbled away without them.

It was Christmas Eve. The boys were bustling about with holly. Darling was perched on a very high chair in the kitchen, picking raisins in the most honourable manner, without eating one, and Madam Liberality ought to have been the happiest of all.

Even now she dried her tears, and made the best of her ill-luck. The sweetmeats were very good; and it was yet in her power to please the others, though by a sacrifice from which she had shrunk. She could divide her scallop-shells among them. It was economy—economy of resources—which made her hesitate. Separated—they would please the boys once, and then be lost. Kept together in her own possession—they would be a constant source of triumph for herself, and of treats for her brothers and sister.

Meanwhile, she would gargle her throat with salt and water. As she crept up-stairs with this purpose, she met her mother.

Madam Liberality had not looked in the looking-glass lately, so she did not understand her mother's exclamation of distress when they met. Her face was perfectly white, except where dark marks lay under her eyes, and her small lips formed between them the rigid line of pain. It was impossible to hold out any longer, and Madam Liberality broke down and poured forth all her woes.

"I'll put my feet in hot water, and do anything you like, mother dear," said she, "if only you'll let me try and have a tree, and keep it secret from the others. I do so want to surprise them."

"If you'll go to your room, my darling, and do as I tell you, I'll keep your secret, and help you with your tree," said her mother. "Don't cry, my child, don't cry; it's so bad for your throat. I think I can find you some beads to make a necklace for Darling, and three pencils for the boys, and some paper which you can cut up into drawing-books for them."

A little hope went a long way with Madam Liberality, and she began to take heart. At the same time she felt her illness more keenly now there was no need for concealing it. She sat over the fire and inhaled steam from an old teapot, and threaded beads, and hoped she would be allowed to go to church next day, and to preside at her Christmas-tree afterwards.

In the afternoon her throat grew rapidly worse. She had begged—almost impatiently—that Darling would not leave the Christmas preparations to sit with her, and as talking was bad for her, and as she had secret preparations to make on her own account, her mother had supported her wish to be left alone.

But when it grew dusk, and the drawing-books were finished, Madam Liberality felt lonely. She put a shawl round her head, and went to the window. There was not much to be seen. The fields were deeply buried in snow, and looked like great white feather beds, shaken up unequally against the hedges. The road was covered so deeply that she could hardly have traced it, if she had not known where it was. How dark the old church tower looked amid so much whiteness!

And the snow-flakes fell like sugar-plums among the black trees. One could almost hear the keen wind rustling through the bending sedges by the pond, where the ice looked quite "safe" now. Madam Liberality hoped she would be able to get out before this fine frost was over. She knew of an old plank which would make an admirable sledge, and she had a plan for the grandest of winter games all ready in her head. It was to be called Arctic Discovery—and she was to be the chief discoverer.

As she fancied herself—starving but scientific, chilled to the bone, yet undaunted—discovering a north-west passage at the upper end of the goose pond, the clock struck three from the old church tower. Madam Liberality heard it with a pang. At three o'clock—if he had had her shillings—she would have been expecting the return of the carrier, with the presents for her Christmas-tree.

Even as she thought about it, the old hooded waggon came lumbering down among the snow-drifts in the lane. There was a bunch of mistletoe at the head, and the old carrier went before the horse, and the dog went before the carrier. And they were all three up to their knees in snow, and all three had their noses down, as much as to say, "Such is life; but we must struggle on."

Poor Madam Liberality! The sight of the waggon and the mistletoe overwhelmed her. It only made matters worse to see the waggon come towards the house. She rather wondered what the carrier was bringing; but whatever it was, it was not the toys.

She went back to her seat by the fire, and cried bitterly; and, as she cried, the ball in her throat seemed to grow larger, till she could hardly breathe. She was glad when the door opened, and her mother's kind face looked in.

"Is Darling here?" she asked.

"No, mother," said Madam Liberality huskily.

"Then you may bring it in," said her mother to some one outside, and the servant appeared, carrying a wooden box, which she put down before Madam Liberality, and then withdrew. "Now don't speak," said her mother, "it is bad for you, and your eyes have asked fifty questions already, my child. Where did the box come from? The carrier brought it. Who is it for? It's for you. Who sent it? That I don't know. What is inside? I thought you would like to be the first to see. My idea is that perhaps your godmother has sent you a Christmas-box, and I thought that there might be things in it which would help you with your Christmas-tree, so I have not told any one about it."

To the end of her life Madam Liberality never forgot that Christmas-box. It did not come from her godmother, and the name of the giver she never knew. The first thing in it was a card, on which was written—"A Christmas-box from an unknown friend;" and the second thing in it was the set of china tea-things with the green rim; and the third thing was a box of doll's furniture.

"Oh, Mother!" cried Madam Liberality, "they're the very things I was counting over in the bazaar, when the shopman heard me."

"Did anybody else hear you?" asked her mother.

"There was a lady, who said, 'I think the little girl said the box of beasts.' And, oh! Mother, Mother! here *is* the box of beasts! They're not common beasts, you know—not wooden ones, painted; they're rough, something like hair. And feel the old elephant's ears, they're quite leathery, and the lion has real long hair for his mane and the tip of his tail. They are such thorough beasts. Oh, how the boys will like them! Tom shall have the darling brown bear. I do think he is the very best beast of all; his mouth is a little open, you know, and you can see his tongue, and it's red. And, Mother! the sheep are curly! And oh, what a dog! with real hair. I think I *must* keep the dog. And I shall make him a paper collar, and print 'Faithful' on it, and let him always stand on the drawers by our bed, and he'll be Darling's and my watch-dog."

Happiness is sometimes very wholesome, but it does not cure a quinsy off hand. Darling cried that night when the big pillow was brought out, which Madam Liberality always slept against in her quinsies, to keep her from choking. She did not know of that consolatory Christmas-box in the cupboard.

On Christmas Day Madam Liberality was speechless. The quinsy had progressed very rapidly.

"It generally breaks the day I have to write on my slate," Madam Liberality wrote, looking up at her mother with piteous eyes.

She was conscious that she had been greatly to blame for what she was suffering, and was anxious to "behave well about it" as an atonement. She begged—on her slate—that no one would stay away from church on her account, but her mother would not leave her.

"And now the others are gone," said Mother, "since you won't let the Christmas-tree be put off, I propose that we have it up, and I dress it under your orders, whilst the others are out, and then it can be moved into the little book-room, all ready for to-night."

Madam Liberality nodded like a china Mandarin.

"But you are in sad pain, I fear?" said her mother,

"One can't have everything," wrote Madam Liberality on her slate. Many illnesses had made her a very philosophical little woman; and, indeed, if the quinsy broke and she were at ease, the combination of good things would be more than any one could reasonably expect, even at Christmas.

Every beast was labelled, and hung up by her orders. The box of furniture was addressed to herself and Darling, as a joint possession, and the sweetmeats were tied in bags of muslin. The tree looked charming. The very angel at the top seemed proud of it.

"I'll leave the tea-things up-stairs," said Mother.

But Madam Liberality shook her head vigorously. She had been making up her mind, as she sat steaming over the old teapot; and now she wrote on her slate, "Put a white cloth round the tub, and put out the tea-things like a tea-party, and put a ticket in the slop-basin—*For Darling. With very*, VERY *Best Love*. Make the last 'very' very big."

Madam Liberality's mother nodded, but she was printing a ticket; much too large a ticket, however, to go into the green and white slop-basin. When it was done she hung it on the tree, under the angel. The inscription was—*From Madam Liberality*.

When supper was over, she came up to Madam Liberality's room, and said,

"Now, my dear, if you like to change your mind and put off the tree till you are better, I will say nothing about it."

But Madam Liberality shook her head more vehemently than before, and her mother smiled and went away.

Madam Liberality strained her ears. The book-room door opened—she knew the voice of the handle—there was a rush and a noise, but it died away into the room. The tears broke down Madam Liberality's cheeks. It was hard not to be there now. Then there was a patter up the stairs, and flying steps along the landing, and Madam Liberality's door was opened by Darling. She was dressed in the pink dress, and her cheeks were pinker still, and her eyes full of tears. And she threw herself at Madam Liberality's feet, crying,

"Oh *how* good, how *very* good you are!"

At this moment a roar came up from below, and Madam Liberality wrote,

"What is it?" and then dropped the slate to clutch the arms of her chair, for the pain was becoming almost intolerable. Before Darling could open the door her mother came in, and Darling repeated the question,

"What is it?"

But at this moment the reply came from below, in Tom's loudest tones. It rang through the house, and up into the bedroom.

"Three cheers for Madam Liberality! Hip, hip, hooray!"

The extremes of pleasure and of pain seemed to meet in Madam Liberality's little head. But overwhelming gratification got the upper hand, and, forgetting even her quinsy, she tried to speak, and after a brief struggle she said, with tolerable distinctness,

"Tell Tom I am very much obliged to him."

But what they did tell Tom was that the quinsy had broken, on which he gave three cheers more.

Juliana Horatia Ewing

PART II

Madam Liberality grew up into much the same sort of person that she was when a child. She always had been what is termed old-fashioned, and the older she grew the better her old-fashionedness became her, so that at last her friends would say to her, "Ah, if we all wore as well as you do, my dear! You've hardly changed at all since we remember you in short petticoats." So far as she did change the change was for the better. (It is to be hoped we do improve a little as we get older!) She was still liberal and economical. She still planned and hoped indefatigably. She was still tender-hearted in the sense in which Gray speaks,

"To each his sufferings, all are men
Condemned alike to groan,
The tender for another's pain,
The unfeeling for his own."

She still had a good deal of ill-health and ill-luck, and a good deal of pleasure in spite of both. She was still happy in the happiness of others, and pleased by their praise. But she was less headstrong and opinionated in her plans, and less fretful when they failed. It is possible, after one has cut one's wisdom-teeth, to cure one's self even of a good deal of vanity, and to learn to play the second fiddle very gracefully; and Madam Liberality did not resist the lessons of life.

GOD teaches us wisdom in divers ways. Why He suffers some people to have so many troubles and so little of what we call pleasure in this world we cannot in this world know. The heaviest blows often fall on the weakest shoulders, and how these endure and bear up under them is another of the things which GOD knows better than we.

I will not pretend to decide whether grown-up people's troubles are harder to bear than children's troubles, but they are of a graver kind. It is very bitter when the boys melt the nose of one's dearest doll against the stove, and living pets with kind eyes and friendly paws grow aged and die; but the death of friends is a more serious and lasting sorrow, if it is not more real.

Madam Liberality shed fewer tears after she grew up than she had done before, but she had some heart-aches which did not heal.

The thing which did most to cure her of being too managing for the good of other people was Darling's marriage. If ever Madam Liberality had felt proud of self-sacrifice and success, it was about this. But when Darling was fairly gone, and "Faithful"—very grey with dust and years—kept watch over only one sister in "the girls' room," he might have seen Madam Liberality's nightly tears if his eyes had been made of anything more sensitive than yellow paint.

Desolate as she was, Madam Liberality would have hugged her grief if she could have had her old consolation, and been happy in the happiness of another. Darling never said she was not happy. It was what she left out, not what she put into the long letters she sent from India that cut Madam Liberality to the heart.

Darling's husband read all her letters, and he did not like the home ones to be too tender—as if Darling's mother and sister pitied her. And he read Darling's letters before they went away by the mail.

From this it came about that the sisters' letters were very commonplace on the surface. And though Madam Liberality cried when Darling wrote, "Have swallows built in the summer-house this year? Have you put my old doll's chest of drawers back in its place since the room was papered? What colour is the paper?"—the Major only said that stuff like that was hardly worth the postage to England. And when Madam Liberality wrote, "The clump of daffodils in your old bed was enormous this spring. I have not touched it since you left. I made Mother's birthday wreath out of the flowers in your bed and mine. Jemima broke the slop-basin of the green and white tea-set to-day. It was the last piece left. I am trying to forgive her,"—the Major made no harsher remark than, "A storm in a slop-basin! Your sister is not a brilliant letter-writer, certainly."

The source of another heart-ache for Madam Liberality was poor Tom. He was as liberal and hospitable as ever in his own way. He invited his friends to stay with his mother, and when they and Tom had gone, Madam Liberality and her mother lived without meat to get the housekeeping book straight again. Their great difficulty in the matter was the uncertain nature of Tom's requirements. And when he did write for money he always wrote in such urgent need that there was no refusing him if by the art of "doing without" his wants could be supplied.

But Tom had a kindly heart; he sent his sister a gold locket, and wrote on the box, "For the best and most generous of sisters."

Madam Liberality liked praise, and she dearly liked praise

from Tom; but on this occasion it failed to soothe her. She said curtly, "I suppose it's not paid for. If we can't afford much, we can afford to live at our own expense, and not on the knavery or the forbearance of tradesmen." With which she threw the locket into a box of odds and ends, and turned the key with some temper.

Years passed, and Madam Liberality was alone. Her mother was dead, and Tom—poor Tom!—had been found drowned. Darling was still in India, and the two living boys were in the colonies, farming.

It seemed to be an aggravation of the calamity of Tom's death that he died, as he had lived, in debt. But, as regards Madam Liberality, it was not an unmixed evil. It is one of our bitterest pangs when we survive those we love that with death the opportunity has passed for being kind to them, though we love them more than ever. By what earthly effort could Madam Liberality's mother now be pleased, whom so little had pleased heretofore?

But for poor Tom it was still possible to plan, to economize, to be liberal—and by these means to pay his debts, and save the fair name of which he had been as reckless as of everything else which he possessed.

Madam Liberality had had many a hard struggle to get Tom a birthday present, but she had never pinched and planned and saved on his behalf as she did now. There is a limit, however, to the strictest economies. It would have taken a longer time to finish her labour of love but for "the other boys." They were good, kind fellows, and having had to earn daily bread where larks do not fall ready cooked into the mouth, they knew more of the realities of life than poor Tom had ever learned. They were prosperous now, and often sent a few pounds to Madam Liberality "to buy a present with."

"And none of your old 'Liberality' tricks, mind!" George wrote on one occasion. "Fit yourself thoroughly out in the latest fashions, and do us credit!"

But it all went to Tom's tailor.

She felt hardly justified in diverting George's money from his purpose; but she had never told the boys of Tom's debts. There was something of her old love of doing things without help in this, and more of her special love for Tom.

It was not from the boys alone that help came to her. Madam Liberality's godmother died, and left her fifty pounds. In one lump she had now got enough to finish her work.

The acknowledgments of these last payments came on Tom's birthday. More and more courteous had grown the tradesmen's letters, and Madam Liberality felt a foolish pleasure in seeing how respectfully they all spoke now of "Your lamented brother, Madam!"

The jeweller's bill was the last; and when Madam Liberality tied up the bundle, she got out Tom's locket and put a bit of his hair into it, and tied it round her throat, sobbing as she did so, "Oh, Tom, if you *could* have lived and been happy in a small way! Your debts are paid now, my poor boy. I wonder if you know. Oh, Tom, Tom!"

It was her greatest triumph—to have saved Tom's fair name in the place where he had lived so foolishly and died so sadly.

But the triumphs of childhood cast fewer shadows. There was no one now to say, "Three cheers for Madam Liberality!"

*   *   *   *   *

It was a very cold winter, but Madam Liberality and Jemima, the maid-of-all-work, were warmer than they had been for several previous winters, because they kept better fires. Time heals our sorrows in spite of us, and Madam Liberality was a very cheerful little body now, and as busy as ever about her Christmas-boxes. Those for her nephews and nieces were already despatched. "The boys" were married; Madam Liberality was godmother to several children she had never seen; but the Benjamin of his aunt's heart was Darling's only child—Tom—though she had not seen even him.

Madam Liberality was still in the thick of her plans, which were chiefly to benefit the old people and the well-behaved children of the village. All the Christmas-boxes were to be "surprises," and Jemima was in every secret but the one which most concerned her.

Madam Liberality had even some plans for her own benefit. George had talked of coming home in the summer, and she began to think of saving up for a new carpet for the drawing-room. Then the last time she went to the town she saw some curtains of a most artistic pattern, and particularly cheap. So much good taste for so little money was rare in provincial shops. By and by she might do without something which would balance the cost of the curtains. And she had another ambition—to provide Jemima with black dresses and white muslin aprons for afternoon wear in addition to her wages, that the outward aspect of that good soul might be more in accordance than hitherto with her intrinsic excellence.

She was pondering this when Jemima burst in in her cooking apron, followed up the passage by the steam of Christmas cakes, and carrying a letter.

"It's a big one, Miss," said she. "Perhaps it's a Christmas-box, Miss." And beaming with geniality and kitchen warmth, Jemima returned to her labours.

Madam Liberality made up her mind about the dresses and aprons; then she opened her letter.

It announced the death of her cousin, her godmother's husband. It announced also that, in spite of the closest search for a will, which he was supposed to have made, this could not be found.

Possibly he had destroyed it, intending to make another. As it was he had died intestate, and succession not being limited to heirs male, and Madam Liberality being the eldest child of his nearest relative—the old childish feeling of its being a dream came over her.

She pinched herself, however, to no purpose. There lay the letter, and after a second reading Madam Liberality picked up the thread of the narrative and arrived at the result—she had inherited fifteen thousand a year.

The first rational idea which came to her was that there was no difficulty now about getting the curtains; and the second was that their chief merit was a merit no more. What is the good of a thing being cheap when one has fifteen thousand a year?

Madam Liberality poked the fire extravagantly, and sat down to think.

The curtains naturally led her to household questions, and those to that invaluable person, Jemima. That Jemima's wages should be doubled, trebled, quadrupled, was a thing of course. What post she was to fill in the new circumstances was another matter. Remembering Podmore, and recalling the fatigue of dressing herself after her pretty numerous illnesses. Madam Liberality felt that a lady's-maid would be a comfort to be most thankful for. But she could not fancy Jemima in that capacity, or as a housekeeper, or even as head housemaid or cook. She had lived for years with Jemima herself, but she could not fit her into a suitable place in the servants' hall.

However, with fifteen thousand a year, Madam Liberality could buy, if needful, a field, and build a house, and put Jemima into it with a servant to wait upon her. The really important question was about her new domestics. Sixteen servants are a heavy responsibility.

Madam Liberality had very high ideas of the parental duties involved in being the head of a household. She had suffered—more than Jemima—over Jemima's lack of scruple as to telling lies for good purposes. Now a footman is a young man who has, no doubt, his own peculiar temptations. What check could Madam Liberality keep upon him? Possibly she might—under the strong pressure of moral responsibility—give good general advice to the footman; but the idea of the butler troubled her.

When one has lived alone in a little house for many years one gets timid. She put a case to herself. Say that she knew the butler to be in the habit of stealing the wine, and suspected the gardener of making a good income by the best of the wall fruit, would she have the moral courage to be as firm with these important personages as if she had caught one of the school-children picking and stealing in the orchard? And if not, would not family prayers be a mockery?

Madam Liberality sighed. Poor dear Tom! He had had his faults certainly; but how well he would have managed a butler!

This touched the weak point of her good fortune to the core. It had come too late to heap luxuries about dear "Mother"; too late to open careers for the boys; too late to give mad frolics and girlish gaieties to light hearts, such as she and Darling had once had. Ah, if they could have enjoyed it together years ago!

There remained, however, Madam Liberality's old consolation: one can be happy in the happiness of others. There were nephews and nieces to be provided for, and a world so full of poor and struggling folk that fifteen thousand a year would only go a little way. It was, perhaps, useful that there had been so many articles lately in the papers about begging letters, and impostors, and, the evil effects of the indiscriminate charity of elderly ladies; but the remembrance of them made Madam Liberality's head ache, and troubled her dreams that night.

It was well that the next day was Sunday. Face to face with those greater interests common to the rich and the poor, the living and the dead, Madam Liberality grew calmer under her new cares and prospects. It did not need that brief pause by her mother's grave to remind her how little money can do for us: and the sight of other people wholesomely recalled how much it can effect. Near the church porch she was passed by the wife of a retired chandler, who dressed in very fine silks, and who was accustomed to eye Madam Liberality's old clothes as she bowed to her more obviously than is consistent with good breeding. The little lady nodded very kindly in return. With fifteen thousand a year one can afford to be *quite* at ease in an old shawl.

The next day was Christmas Eve. Madam Liberality caught herself thinking that if the legacy had been smaller—say fifty pounds a year—she would at once have treated herself to certain little embellishments of the old house, for which she had long been ambitious. But it would be absurd to buy two or three yards of rosebud chintz, and tire herself by making covers to two very old sofa-cushions, when the point to be decided was in which of three grandly furnished mansions she would first take up her abode. She ordered a liberal supper, however, which confirmed Jemima in her secret opinion that the big letter had brought good news.

When, therefore, another letter of similar appearance arrived, Jemima snatched up the waiter and burst breathlessly in upon Madam Liberality, leaving the door open-behind her, though it was bitterly cold and the snow fell fast.

And when Madam Liberality opened this letter she learned that her cousin's will had been found, and that (as seems to be natural) he had left his money where it would be associated with more money and kept well together. His heir was a cousin also, but in the next degree—an old bachelor, who was already wealthy; and he had left Madam Liberality five pounds to buy a mourning ring.

It had been said that Madam Liberality was used to disappointment, but some minutes passed before she quite realized the downfall of her latest visions. Then the old sofa-cushions resumed their importance, and she flattened the fire into a more economical shape, and set vigorously to work to decorate the house with the Christmas evergreens. She had just finished and gone up-stairs to wash her hands when the church clock struck three.

It was an old house, and the window of the bedroom went down to the floor, and had a deep window-seat. Madam Liberality sat down in it and looked out. She expected some linsey-woolsey by the carrier, to make Christmas petticoats, and she was glad to see the hooded waggon ploughing its way through the snow. The goose-pond was firmly frozen, and everything looked as it had looked years ago, except that the carrier's young son went before the waggon and a young dog went before him. They passed slowly out of sight, but Madam Liberality sat on. She gazed dreamily at the old church, and the trees, and the pond, and thought of the past; of her mother, and of poor Tom, and of Darling, and she thought till she fancied that she heard Darling's voice in the passage below. She got up to go down to Jemima, but as she did so she heard a footstep on the stairs, and it was not Jemima's tread. It was too light for the step of any man or woman.

Then the door opened, and on the threshold of Madam Liberality's room stood a little boy dressed in black, with his little hat pushed back from the loveliest of baby faces set in long flaxen hair. The carnation colour of his cheeks was deepened by the frost, and his bright eyes were brighter from mingled daring and doubt and curiosity, as he looked leisurely round the room and said in a slow, high-pitched, and very distinct tone,

"Where are you, Aunt Liberality?"

But, lovely as he was, Madam Liberality ran past him, for another figure was in the doorway now, also in black, and, with a widow's cap; and Madam Liberality and Darling fell sobbing into each other's arms.

"This is better than fifteen thousand a year," said Madam Liberality.

* * * * *

It is not necessary to say much more. The Major had been killed by a fall from horseback, and Darling came back to live at her old home. She had a little pension, and the sisters were not parted again.

It would be idle to dwell on Madam Liberality's devotion to her nephew, or the princely manner in which he accepted her services. That his pleasure was the object of a new series of plans, and presents, and surprises, will be readily understood. The curtains were bought, but the new carpet had to be deferred in consequence of an extravagant outlay on mechanical toys. When the working of these brought a deeper tint into his cheeks, and a brighter light into his eyes, Madam Liberality was quite happy; and when he broke them one after another, his infatuated aunt believed this to be a precocious development of manly energies.

The longest lived, if not the favourite, toys with him were the old set of scallop-shells, with which he never wearied of making feasts, to which Madam Liberality was never weary of being invited. He had more plums than had ever sweetened her childhood, and when they sat together on two footstools by the sofa, and Tom announced the contents of the dishes in his shrillest voice and lifted the covers, Madam Liberality would say in a tone of apology,

"It's very odd, Darling, and I'm sure at my time of life it's disgraceful, but I cannot feel old!"

We could hardly take leave of Madam Liberality in pleasanter circumstances. Why should we ask whether, for the rest of her life, she was rich or poor, when we may feel so certain that she was contented? No doubt she had many another hope and disappointment to keep life from stagnating.

As a matter of fact she outlived the bachelor cousin, and if he died intestate she must have been rich after all. Perhaps she was. Perhaps she never suffered again from insufficient food or warmth. Perhaps the illnesses of her later years were alleviated by skill and comforts such as hitherto she had never known. Perhaps Darling and she enjoyed a sort of second spring in their old age, and went every year to the Continent, and grew wonderful flowers in the greenhouse, and sent Tom to Eton, and provided for their nephews and nieces, and built churches to their mother's memory, and never had to withhold the liberal hand from helping because it was empty; and so passed by a time of wealth to the hour of death.

Or perhaps the cousin took good care to bequeath his money where there was more money for it to stick to. And Madam Liberality pinched out her little presents as heretofore, and kept herself warm with a hot bottle when she could not afford a fire, and was too thankful to have Darling with her when she was ill to want anything else. And perhaps Darling and she prepared Tom for school, and (like many another widow's son) he did them credit. And perhaps they were quite happy with a few common pot-plants in the sunny window, and kept their mother's memory green by flowers about her grave, and so passed by a life of small cares and small pleasures to where

"Divided households re-unite."

Of one thing we may be quite certain. Rich or poor, she was always

MADAM LIBERALITY

Choose from Thousands of 1stWorldLibrary Classics By

A. M. Barnard
Ada Leverson
Adolphus William Ward
Aesop
Agatha Christie
Alexander Aaronsohn
Alexander Kielland
Alexandre Dumas
Alfred Gatty
Alfred Ollivant
Alice Duer Miller
Alice Turner Curtis
Alice Dunbar
Allen Chapman
Alleyne Ireland
Ambrose Bierce
Amelia E. Barr
Amory H. Bradford
Andrew Lang
Andrew McFarland Davis
Andy Adams
Angela Brazil
Anna Alice Chapin
Anna Sewell
Annie Besant
Annie Hamilton Donnell
Annie Payson Call
Annie Roe Carr
Annonaymous
Anton Chekhov
Archibald Lee Fletcher
Arnold Bennett
Arthur C. Benson
Arthur Conan Doyle
Arthur M. Winfield
Arthur Ransome
Arthur Schnitzler
Arthur Train
Atticus
B.H. Baden-Powell
B. M. Bower
B. C. Chatterjee
Baroness Emmuska Orczy
Baroness Orczy
Basil King
Bayard Taylor
Ben Macomber
Bertha Muzzy Bower
Bjornstjerne Bjornson

Booth Tarkington
Boyd Cable
Bram Stoker
C. Collodi
C. E. Orr
C. M. Ingleby
Carolyn Wells
Catherine Parr Traill
Charles A. Eastman
Charles Amory Beach
Charles Dickens
Charles Dudley Warner
Charles Farrar Browne
Charles Ives
Charles Kingsley
Charles Klein
Charles Hanson Towne
Charles Lathrop Pack
Charles Romyn Dake
Charles Whibley
Charles Willing Beale
Charlotte M. Braeme
Charlotte M. Yonge
Charlotte Perkins Stetson
Clair W. Hayes
Clarence Day Jr.
Clarence E. Mulford
Clemence Housman
Confucius
Coningsby Dawson
Cornelis DeWitt Wilcox
Cyril Burleigh
D. H. Lawrence
Daniel Defoe
David Garnett
Dinah Craik
Don Carlos Janes
Donald Keyhoe
Dorothy Kilner
Dougan Clark
Douglas Fairbanks
E. Nesbit
E. P. Roe
E. Phillips Oppenheim
E. S. Brooks
Earl Barnes
Edgar Rice Burroughs
Edith Van Dyne
Edith Wharton

Edward Everett Hale
Edward J. O'Biren
Edward S. Ellis
Edwin L. Arnold
Eleanor Atkins
Eleanor Hallowell Abbott
Eliot Gregory
Elizabeth Gaskell
Elizabeth McCracken
Elizabeth Von Arnim
Ellem Key
Emerson Hough
Emilie F. Carlen
Emily Bronte
Emily Dickinson
Enid Bagnold
Enilor Macartney Lane
Erasmus W. Jones
Ernie Howard Pie
Ethel May Dell
Ethel Turner
Ethel Watts Mumford
Eugene Sue
Eugenie Foa
Eugene Wood
Eustace Hale Ball
Evelyn Everett-green
Everard Cotes
F. H. Cheley
F. J. Cross
F. Marion Crawford
Fannie E. Newberry
Federick Austin Ogg
Ferdinand Ossendowski
Fergus Hume
Florence A. Kilpatrick
Fremont B. Deering
Francis Bacon
Francis Darwin
Frances Hodgson Burnett
Frances Parkinson Keyes
Frank Gee Patchin
Frank Harris
Frank Jewett Mather
Frank L. Packard
Frank V. Webster
Frederic Stewart Isham
Frederick Trevor Hill
Frederick Winslow Taylor

Friedrich Kerst	Hayden Carruth	James Branch Cabell
Friedrich Nietzsche	Helent Hunt Jackson	James DeMille
Fyodor Dostoyevsky	Helen Nicolay	James Joyce
G.A. Henty	Hendrik Conscience	James Lane Allen
G.K. Chesterton	Hendy David Thoreau	James Lane Allen
Gabrielle E. Jackson	Henri Barbusse	James Oliver Curwood
Garrett P. Serviss	Henrik Ibsen	James Oppenheim
Gaston Leroux	Henry Adams	James Otis
George A. Warren	Henry Ford	James R. Driscoll
George Ade	Henry Frost	Jane Abbott
Geroge Bernard Shaw	Henry James	Jane Austen
George Cary Eggleston	Henry Jones Ford	Jane L. Stewart
George Durston	Henry Seton Merriman	Janet Aldridge
George Ebers	Henry W Longfellow	Jens Peter Jacobsen
George Eliot	Herbert A. Giles	Jerome K. Jerome
George Gissing	Herbert Carter	Jessie Graham Flower
George MacDonald	Herbert N. Casson	John Buchan
George Meredith	Herman Hesse	John Burroughs
George Orwell	Hildegard G. Frey	John Cournos
George Sylvester Viereck	Homer	John F. Kennedy
George Tucker	Honore De Balzac	John Gay
George W. Cable	Horace B. Day	John Glasworthy
George Wharton James	Horace Walpole	John Habberton
Gertrude Atherton	Horatio Alger Jr.	John Joy Bell
Gordon Casserly	Howard Pyle	John Kendrick Bangs
Grace E. King	Howard R. Garis	John Milton
Grace Gallatin	Hugh Lofting	John Philip Sousa
Grace Greenwood	Hugh Walpole	John Taintor Foote
Grant Allen	Humphry Ward	Jonas Lauritz Idemil Lie
Guillermo A. Sherwell	Ian Maclaren	Jonathan Swift
Gulielma Zollinger	Inez Haynes Gillmore	Joseph A. Altsheler
Gustav Flaubert	Irving Bacheller	Joseph Carey
H. A. Cody	Isabel Cecilia Williams	Joseph Conrad
H. B. Irving	Isabel Hornibrook	Joseph E. Badger Jr
H.C. Bailey	Israel Abrahams	Joseph Hergesheimer
H. G. Wells	Ivan Turgenev	Joseph Jacobs
H. H. Munro	J.G.Austin	Jules Vernes
H. Irving Hancock	J. Henri Fabre	Julian Hawthrone
H. R. Naylor	J. M. Barrie	Julie A Lippmann
H. Rider Haggard	J. M. Walsh	Justin Huntly McCarthy
H. W. C. Davis	J. Macdonald Oxley	Kakuzo Okakura
Haldeman Julius	J. R. Miller	Karle Wilson Baker
Hall Caine	J. S. Fletcher	Kate Chopin
Hamilton Wright Mabie	J. S. Knowles	Kenneth Grahame
Hans Christian Andersen	J. Storer Clouston	Kenneth McGaffey
Harold Avery	J. W. Duffield	Kate Langley Bosher
Harold McGrath	Jack London	Kate Langley Bosher
Harriet Beecher Stowe	Jacob Abbott	Katherine Cecil Thurston
Harry Castlemon	James Allen	Katherine Stokes
Harry Coghill	James Andrews	L. A. Abbot
Harry Houidini	James Baldwin	L. T. Meade

L. Frank Baum
Latta Griswold
Laura Dent Crane
Laura Lee Hope
Laurence Housman
Lawrence Beasley
Leo Tolstoy
Leonid Andreyev
Lewis Carroll
Lewis Sperry Chafer
Lilian Bell
Lloyd Osbourne
Louis Hughes
Louis Joseph Vance
Louis Tracy
Louisa May Alcott
Lucy Fitch Perkins
Lucy Maud Montgomery
Luther Benson
Lydia Miller Middleton
Lyndon Orr
M. Corvus
M. H. Adams
Margaret E. Sangster
Margret Howth
Margaret Vandercook
Margaret W. Hungerford
Margret Penrose
Maria Edgeworth
Maria Thompson Daviess
Mariano Azuela
Marion Polk Angellotti
Mark Overton
Mark Twain
Mary Austin
Mary Catherine Crowley
Mary Cole
Mary Hastings Bradley
Mary Roberts Rinehart
Mary Rowlandson
M. Wollstonecraft Shelley
Maud Lindsay
Max Beerbohm
Myra Kelly
Nathaniel Hawthrone
Nicolo Machiavelli
O. F. Walton
Oscar Wilde

Owen Johnson
P.G. Wodehouse
Paul and Mabel Thorne
Paul G. Tomlinson
Paul Severing
Percy Brebner
Percy Keese Fitzhugh
Peter B. Kyne
Plato
Quincy Allen
R. Derby Holmes
R. L. Stevenson
R. S. Ball
Rabindranath Tagore
Rahul Alvares
Ralph Bonehill
Ralph Henry Barbour
Ralph Victor
Ralph Waldo Emmerson
Rene Descartes
Ray Cummings
Rex Beach
Rex E. Beach
Richard Harding Davis
Richard Jefferies
Richard Le Gallienne
Robert Barr
Robert Frost
Robert Gordon Anderson
Robert L. Drake
Robert Lansing
Robert Lynd
Robert Michael Ballantyne
Robert W. Chambers
Rosa Nouchette Carey
Rudyard Kipling
Saint Augustine
Samuel B. Allison
Samuel Hopkins Adams
Sarah Bernhardt
Sarah C. Hallowell
Selma Lagerlof
Sherwood Anderson
Sigmund Freud
Standish O'Grady
Stanley Weyman
Stella Benson
Stella M. Francis

Stephen Crane
Stewart Edward White
Stijn Streuvels
Swami Abhedananda
Swami Parmananda
T. S. Ackland
T. S. Arthur
The Princess Der Ling
Thomas A. Janvier
Thomas A Kempis
Thomas Anderton
Thomas Bailey Aldrich
Thomas Bulfinch
Thomas De Quincey
Thomas Dixon
Thomas H. Huxley
Thomas Hardy
Thomas More
Thornton W. Burgess
U. S. Grant
Upton Sinclair
Valentine Williams
Various Authors
Vaughan Kester
Victor Appleton
Victor G. Durham
Victoria Cross
Virginia Woolf
Wadsworth Camp
Walter Camp
Walter Scott
Washington Irving
Wilbur Lawton
Wilkie Collins
Willa Cather
Willard F. Baker
William Dean Howells
William le Queux
W. Makepeace Thackeray
William W. Walter
William Shakespeare
Winston Churchill
Yei Theodora Ozaki
Yogi Ramacharaka
Young E. Allison
Zane Grey